I'm Sending a Shamrock to Remind You of Home
Roscommon Families and the Irish Diaspora 1875-1950

Thomas Callahan, Jr.

Rider University

GLASNEVIN
PUBLISHING

First published in 2013 by

Glasnevin Publishing, 2nd Floor,
13 Upper Baggot Street, Dublin 4, Ireland
www.glasnevinpublishing.com

based in Dublin, UNESCO City of Literature

A CIP catalogue record for this book is available from the British Library

Papers used by Glasnevin Publishing are from well managed forests
and other responsible sources.

ISBN: 978-1-908689-23-8

To
Ellen and Patty
For Their Love and Support

Contents

Acknowledgments

This book would not have been possible without much assistance from family, friends and colleagues, both here and in Ireland. Though I cannot name them all here, I would like to especially thank a few whose help and encouragement supported me over the past couple of years and made this book much better than it otherwise would have been.

First, I thank Rider University for awarding me the research leave that afforded me the time and freedom to concentrate on my research for this study. Having a block of time that I could devote exclusively to family papers, genealogical and archival records greatly hastened the completion of this study.

My new-found McCormack and McLoughlin cousins provided all of the non-archival family documents, photographs and lore that made it possible to reconstruct the lives of our 19th and early-20th century ancestors. My first contact with Grace McCormack two decades ago launched my investigation, and later correspondence with her sister Jeanne McCormack Lechner provided me with names and evidence which soon led to my meeting Patricia McCormick Davis, who has never forgotten anything she ever heard about family history and who has preserved a treasure trove of family photographs and documents. Without her help this work would be much different and not nearly as good. Thanks go as well to the McCormack descendents still in Ireland whose friendship and generosity made my research trips there productive and pleasant. I owe special thanks to Catherine Carr and her siblings for their hospitality, in particular her brothers John and James for information on and tours of the "homeplace" in Frenchpark. I owe a debt as well to Tom and Ann McLoughlin for their hospitality and for putting me in touch with Sr Joseph [Bridget] McLoughlin who, along with Mai McCormack Robinson are the last surviving members of the previous generation. Their generosity and memories of their parents, aunts and uncles, stretching back over eight decades, are priceless. I also owe debts of gratitude to my colleagues Brooke Hunter, Tom Anthony and

Joe Gowaskie whose constructive criticism of earlier drafts were of great benefit, and to my friend Howard Van Loan whose generous and insightful comments rivaled the length of the manuscript.

Above all, I need to thank my wife Ellen, who gladly read all the drafts and whose suggestions greatly improved them. Her aid with my archival research both here and in Ireland was invaluable and her constant encouragement and steadfast conviction that I could actually write this have sustained me.

Preface

In the second half of the Nineteenth Century millions of Irish men and women fled their homeland for new lives elsewhere. Many were attracted by the promise of a better future in England, Canada, America and Australia, but even more emigrated because they had no other choice. Ireland was still overwhelmingly rural, and the growing trend against farm subdivision meant that most sons faced bleak prospects of inheriting land and establishing families. The stunning success of English industry had resulted in a disastrous loss of jobs for men in Irish cities, and throughout the country young women confronted declining possibilities of marriage.

The first mass emigration had come during The Famine in mid-century when over a million Irish were encouraged or forced to leave home. Landlords evicted many, others left voluntarily. Passage abroad was disorderly and dangerous. Poor, often ill, Irish men, women and families arrived by the hundreds every day in Canada, New York, Boston, and elsewhere, their destination often determined by what ticket was the cheapest. At first, that usually meant Canada, though thousands of these passengers subsequently walked to the United States. Many of these early arrivals found acceptance elusive because of their poverty and their Catholic faith. Still, over the next few decades, these exiles settled into their new lives and sent letters and remittances home to their kin. They became the foundation for future waves of Irish emigrants.

Later in the century, though the horror of The Famine had faded, Ireland's prospects had not much improved. Agitation flared up against grasping landlords and continued localized crop failures precipitated hunger and deprivation. The birthrate remained high, and tillage farming further declined in favor of livestock grazing, making jobs for rural laborers increasingly scarce. More and more, young Irish saw no future for themselves at home. From abroad, however, came letters promising bright prospects for men with strong backs and women with domestic skills. It was said that in America industrial jobs abounded, and young Irish women could easily find work as domestics in the growing middle class households. The advent of safe, rapid steamships cut the journeys abroad by more than half. Fares were low and affordable. Families regularly saw their young, single children depart, most never to return, but many to send money home to those who stayed. Brothers and sisters sent pre-paid tickets to their siblings; often, whole neighborhoods were transplanted across the Atlantic.

This book studies this Irish Diaspora to America through the lens of two generations of one such family, the McCormacks of rural County Roscommon. The parents, survivors of The Famine, had twelve children between 1862 and 1886, ten of whom grew to adulthood. Six of these, four brothers and two sisters, came to America between 1886 and 1901, establishing families that set down roots in northern New Jersey and upstate New York. Four others, three brothers and a sister, stayed home. Taken together, these siblings, their children, friends and neighbors embody the turbulent and intriguing history of the Irish at home and in America from the mid-19th to the mid-20th centuries.

In addition to investigating the Irish Diaspora, the study also addresses the problems facing those who undertake such a project – to recover from obscurity the lives of average people. Unlike public figures and the wealthy who leave memoirs and other written evidence behind them, ordinary folks fade away once living memory forgets them. A few letters, perhaps some snapshots, a wallet someone kept when mom or dad died – these are often all that seemingly remains. But even average people leave a trail if you know where to look and how to use available resources. This book demonstrates the possibilities of such an enterprise.

Catherine Keenan McCormack with Children Catherine and Martin c. 1890

Prologue
An American Wake

On a chilly early-April day in 1897, 20-year old Katie McCormack slowly made the rounds of her Slieveroe townland near Frenchpark in County Roscommon in preparation for yet another "American wake" for the McCormack family. She and her mother, as well as her sisters Bridget and Maggie, had been baking for days, and their neighbors would contribute poitin and porter. Four of her older brothers had already bid their family and friends farewell and set sail for America to begin new lives. As the eldest daughter in the large rural family, Kate had helped her mother keep the small two-room cottage and look after her brothers and younger sisters. But now she too was leaving. Her mother Catherine would be in good hands. James and Martin would help her father look after the farm, while Bridget and little Maggie kept house and worked on the land as well.

As was the tradition, Katie proceeded from cottage to cottage, bidding the Mahons and Farrells farewell, promising Pat Deignan to take a message to his son Peter in America, and hugged and kissed her friends and cousins. Her steamer trunk with her name newly stenciled on the end was packed and ready. Catherine, nearing 60, had already seen four of her ten surviving children perform this ritual and depart over the past decade, but this time was different. Kate was her eldest daughter, her namesake. Though she had known for years that this parting would probably come, it was still wrenching. As evening approached, it was time to escort Katie to Tibohine for a final church service and to receive Fr. McDermott's blessing. Then came the wake — really more of a party, yet not unlike the bittersweet farewells to her two infant sons who had died before their time. Neighbors and relatives crowded into the small cottage, beer and whisky flowed, music and dancing lasted until dawn. All in attendance were determined to make the best of this departure. They knew Katie would be well cared for in America; brothers John, Patrick, Thomas and Michael were solidly established in West Orange, New Jersey, two married and with families already begun. Katie was excited to be going, yet sad and apprehensive too. She had read and re-read her brothers' letters describing America and the opportunities ahead; still it was painful to leave behind all she had known and loved.

In the morning the priest came to the cottage for a final blessing, and the neighbors gathered to "convoy" her to the townland border. Her parents, brothers and sisters would accompany her all the way to the train in Boyle. Trying not to cry too much, she hugged and kissed her family, clung to her mother one last time and promised to write and to be a good girl. She told Catherine that she would return someday, though they both knew in their hearts that they would never meet again. Trunk loaded on the train, it was time for a final embrace. Be good, be well ... God speed. Now, alone for the first time in her life, Kate McCormack was off to Dublin and thence to Queenstown, the RMS Campania and the beginning of her new life.

Chapter 1
Family Origins

The most famous and tragic event in Irish history is The Famine,
or the Great Hunger, as it is often called in Ireland. It ended an
era of rural life and ushered in momentous social changes. When
it began, the founders of the Slieveroe branch of the McCormack
family of Frenchpark in County Roscommon, Patrick
McCormack and Catherine Keenan, were children. They
survived, but it had not been easy. Roscommon, in Connacht,
was one of the areas hardest hit when the potato crop failed.
Well over half the population had at some point received
whatever meager food relief that had been distributed and, when
the immediate crisis had passed, the population had declined by
over 30% from 1844.[1] Though more fertile than in the far west, in
Mayo and Galway, the land around Frenchpark was marginal
for tillage. Over previous generations most farmers there had
come to rely heavily on the potato as their family's principal or
even sole food. Potatoes would grow in poor soil, took little
work to cultivate, and were very nutritious. One could feed a
large number of people from even a small patch of potatoes. This
had encouraged poor families to subdivide their holdings into
ever smaller plots, to provide for their children who could then
marry early. The resulting large families had led to a precarious
situation; if the potato failed, disaster would follow. This is
precisely what happened between 1845 and 1852.

The onset was sudden and catastrophic. There had been
previous periodic small disruptions in the potato harvest, but by
1847 the crop had completely failed. A potato blight had come
initially from America to England, and was then carried by wind
and insects to Ireland. Potatoes rotted in the fields, leaving poor

---

[1] For overview of The Famine's impact in Connacht and the west see Kerby
Miller, *Emigrants and Exiles* (Oxford: Oxford University Press, 1985), 280-353;
David Fitzpatrick, "Emigration 1871-1921," in *A New History of Ireland*, ed. W. E.
Vaughn (Oxford: Clarendon Press, 1996), VI, 607-637; also, Timothy Guinnane,
The Vanishing Irish (Princeton: Princeton University Press),1997.

Irish farmers desperate for food. The initial response of the British government had been generous and fairly effective. Prime Minister Peel, who had personal experience in Irish administration, imported large amounts of corn from the United States, and impending starvation was averted. His generosity, however, brought down his government, and the Whigs in Parliament then instituted a series of largely disastrous measures to deal with the crisis. The new government was particularly enamored of *laissez faire* economic theories. They believed that government should not interfere with the free workings of the market and should especially not promote idleness and inefficiency. Many English liberals, while they might sympathize with starving Irish peasants, were convinced that simply giving them food and other aid would only prolong a society that was hopelessly out of date and doomed to failure. If the Irish were to receive aid, they must work for it. Useless road and wall building schemes were implemented to provide work and wages so that the Irish could buy food. Within a few months even the Whigs realized the folly of this approach, as weakened Irish peasants collapsed on the roadworks and fought among themselves to get the meager wages that were advanced. The British government then initiated a new policy to save the British rate payers money: Irish landlords and Irish money, not the English taxpayer, must fund the relief efforts. This, they concluded, would force Irish landlords finally to carry out thoroughgoing land reform, clear off unproductive tenants and make Irish lands profitable.

With little direct aid coming from England, Irish landlords were increasingly hard-pressed to deal with their tenants. With few crops to be sold, rents went unpaid, and the prospect of landowner bankruptcy loomed ever larger. Local relief commissions were soon overwhelmed. On 23 April 1846 Reverend John French, who owned most of Frenchpark and much other land in the county, informed the Secretary of the Relief Committee For Ireland that local conditions were becoming dire. "A crisis may arise in the town [as a result of] scarcity and want. Meal and potatoes [are being] stored up in various places in the county to be kept for high prices. ... The poor of the town will not be able to purchase [food] even if the present prices continue.... Even Indian meal, at cost price ... is too expensive."[2]

Soon violence grew with people's desperation. In Strokestown, less than twenty miles from Frenchpark, a landlord, Major Denis Mahon was shot dead in 1847 by some of his tenants on his way home from a Relief Commission meeting in Roscommon town.[3] Mahon and many other landlords had seized upon eviction as their best option to avoid bankruptcy: clear off the poor and unproductive peasants and convert their lands to larger, economically viable farms and grazing pastures. Some landlords paid the passages of the evicted farmers to England, Canada or the United States. Others simply had their agents call the constables, turn their tenants out onto the road and immediately pull down their cottages, preventing them from possibly sneaking back. These land clearances not only dealt with the immediate crisis of The Famine, but from the landlords' point of view were also steps toward a solution to a larger problem. English authorities and Anglo-Irish landowners had long decried the overcrowding of rural Ireland; something had to be done or the impending Malthusian nightmare would consume everyone. Some officials like Charles Trevelyan, now the British minister in charge of Irish relief, saw The Famine, not simply as a disaster for the Irish people, but also as a divine intervention. He saw Ireland's main problem as overpopulation and that "...the cure has been applied by the direct stroke of an all-wise Providence in a manner as unexpected and un-thought of as it is likely to be effectual."[4] Such attitudes, however misguided, but sincere, earned the English the enduring hatred

[2] John French, Famine Relief Commission Papers 1844-1847. Ancestry.com http://search.ancestry.com/iexec?htx=View&r=an&dbid= 1772&iid=25_1700_1749-00138&fn=&ln=Rev+John+French&st=r&ssrc=& pid =2116 (accessed 17 February 2013).

[3] Peter Duffy, *The Killing of Major Denis Mahon* (New York: Harper Collins, 2007), 150-154.

[4] J. Ranelagh, *A Short History of Ireland* (Cambridge: Cambridge University Press, 1995), 116.

of the Irish, both at home and abroad. The English had hardly
been popular in Ireland before The Famine, but the government's
slow and seemingly hard-hearted response to the crisis led many
Irish to blame them for the disaster. Many English citizens,
including Queen Victoria herself, had contributed generously to
relief efforts, but the damage to England's reputation was now
irreparable.

Ireland's population, which had stood at slightly over eight
million in the 1841 census, plummeted over the next decade.
Slightly under a million and a half died, mostly from disease
made worse by malnutrition, and a further million and a half
emigrated, mainly to America and British Canada. All told, this
decade saw more Irish leave home than in the previous 250
years.[5]

Now, a little over a decade later, Patrick McCormack and
Catherine Keenan were about to marry and start a family. No
one now knows how they met, but it is probable, considering the
close-knit society of rural Ireland, that they had known each
other since childhood. Their marriage had undoubtedly been
arranged by their parents; a modest dowry had been agreed
upon, and Catherine and Patrick became man and wife in the
little stone chapel at Ballinameen in February of 1861. He was 28
and she was 19.[6] They settled in at a small farm in the townland
of Slieveroe in Frenchpark, County Roscommon.

They rented their modest holding from The Right Honorable
and Reverend Lord John French, 2nd Baron de Freyne of
Coolavin, who had inherited his title from his late brother Arthur
in 1856. The Frenches, to put it mildly, were a wealthy family
who had been major landowners in Roscommon since the 17th
Century. Frenchpark is named after them. John owned over
25,000 acres in County Roscommon, seven of which were rented
to the McCormacks according to the 1857 *Primary Valuation of*

---

[5] Miller, *Emigrants and Exiles*, 291.

[6] Patrium McCormack/Catherinam Keenan marriage record, Ballinameen Parish,
Co. Roscommon, 12 February 1861; LDS Film 989738, Batch M701931.

Tenements, more commonly known as Griffith's Valuation after Richard Griffith, the survey's director.[7] This property evaluation was the most significant land tax survey ever undertaken in Ireland. Conducted between 1847 and 1864, the project was intended to sort out who owned what and to put an accurate rental value on all the land in Ireland for the purpose of assessing various local taxes.

It was a massive project. Evaluators underwent rigorous training designed by Griffith himself to ensure a consistency of results across all the counties. When the survey was ultimately printed, it filled over 300 thick volumes. Each property was listed with landlords, tenants and sub-tenants, along with descriptions of the houses, out-buildings, quality of the land and annual rental value so that accurate local taxes could be assessed each year. In a way it was a worthy successor to the Domesday Book survey ordered by William the Conqueror in the late-11th Century to find out what his newly conquered realm of England was actually worth.

There are also earlier surviving land assessments for Slieveroe from the mid-1820s and early-1830s, contained in the *Tithe Applotment Books*, but no McCormacks appear in Slieveroe in these records. So Griffith's survey is about as far back as the McCormack family can be reliably traced. There are, however, some intriguing possibilities. For example, in the townland of Runnabehy in 1824 tithe is assessed on three McCormacks, Darby, Patrick and James. Birth and baptismal records are rare before the mid-19th century. There were no civil records for Catholics before 1864, so what exists today depends on the haphazard survival of local parish records. We have no way of knowing if any of these men is a direct ancestor, but the townland is but a stone's throw from Slieveroe. By the time of Griffith's survey, some thirty years later, there were no McCormack landholders in Runnabehy. It's certainly possible

---

[7] McCormack, Cath., *Griffith's Valuation*, 1857; Sheet 9, 8, Map reference 5 A, B, no. 26.

that the family had moved the short distance to Slieveroe. Unfortunately, unlike the Irish census records, Griffith's Valuation did not list who actually lived in the renters' households, but only the person responsible for paying the rent. The census surveys, introduced in 1821 and taken every decade, were designed to record the personal information on Ireland's inhabitants. Unfortunately, the vast majority of these records have not survived. During World War I the British government pulped the census tallies from 1861 to 1891 and when the Irish Public Record Office in Dublin's Four Courts complex was burned during the civil war in 1922, all the census records from 1821 to 1851 were also destroyed, leaving Griffith's valuation as the most valuable source for investigating conditions in the immediate post famine period.

A note of caution before proceeding: there are many McCormacks listed in the Griffith's survey of Roscommon. Though the name had disappeared in Runnabehy, a number lived in the townland of Cloonargid, and even more in Kiltybranks, closer to Ballaghadereen than to Frenchpark, and are probably related in some way. This group is of particular interest because some of the family forenames appear, including the very common Patrick, but also Michael, the very popular William, and even a William Martin, both of which names were given to Patrick's and Catherine's sons.[8]

More is known about the Keenan side of the family. Catherine Keenan, born around 1842, was the younger sister of James Keenan from Slieveroe's neighboring townland of Cloonmaguinane. He was eight years Catherine's senior, and their parents were James Keenan and Bridget McGlynn. They, too, were poor tenants of Reverend French and owned no land of their own.[9]

In hopes of delineating a direct family line, I focused on the McCormacks in Slieveroe, where the family homestead still

---

[8] McCormacks, *Griffith's Valuation*; 1857, Sheets 13/14, Map Reference 23, Nos. 5-12.

[9] National Archives of Ireland, 1901, Cloonmagunnaun, House #6.

exists. The landholder there in 1857 was one Catherine McCormack, who had two sub-tenants, Martin Brennan and Michael Farrell. She owed a rent of £2/year and they owed an additional £1.5/year each, for which she was ultimately responsible, making her effective obligation £5/year.[10] The farm was a very modest property. Irish farmers were generally classified as "small farmers" if they held between 5 and 30 acres, and "strong farmers" if over 30 acres. Below 5 acres qualified one as a "cottier" or "laborer." So, renting just seven acres made the McCormacks very small farmers indeed. The amount of rent, however, suggests that the quality of the land was probably good. Since this is the same land that was later held by Patrick and Catherine Keenan McCormack, it is very likely that the Catherine in the 1857 survey was a widow and Patrick's mother. Most likely she died soon thereafter, willing her holding to her son who could then marry and start his own family.

Just a little over a year after their marriage, Patrick and Catherine's first child, John, was born. Eleven others followed, eight boys and three girls, during the next twenty-four years. The eighth of these children and their first daughter, Catherine, was my grandmother.

I remember her, though dimly, since I was only seven when she died. As I grew up I always knew she was Irish, as was her husband Patrick Callahan, but the family never talked about Ireland or being of Irish descent. My father, aunts and uncles did not talk much at all about the past, at least to me, and I was never curious enough to ask about our family's "roots." As time and relatives passed on, Ireland faded farther from family memory. In my father's generation of nine children, only four married, producing a total of five grandchildren for Catherine and Patrick. Over the years, my first cousins and I stalwartly carried on the family disinterest in our own past.

---

[10] McCormack, Cath., *Griffith's Valuation,* 1857; Sheet 9, 8, Map reference 5 A, B: no. 26.

The genesis of this study began with a 1982 vacation that my wife Ellen and I took to England and Ireland. As we were preparing for the trip, I remembered that I had inherited my grandmother's 1928 United States passport that listed her place of birth in Ireland as Frenchpark. Where was this, and were we going to be anywhere near there? I discovered that Frenchpark was a small village in rural County Roscommon in north-central Ireland. The guidebooks ignored it, as did most tourists. Still, Ireland is a compact country, and the drive from Cashel, where we were staying, to the McCormack "home town" was only an hour or two, depending on how many sheep or cattle were blocking the rural roads. So we headed north to see where Catherine McCormack had been born.

In 1837 Samuel Lewis in his *Topographical Dictionary of Ireland* described Frenchpark as a "...market and post-town ... at the junction of the roads from Elphin, Boyle, Castlerea and Ballaghadereen, containing 76 homes and 447 inhabitants."[11] The town had a long and distinguished history, with a remarkable cave perhaps from the days of the druids, and the ruins of Clonshanville Abbey, dating from the 14th century. In present times, he wrote, the future looked bright for the town now that a mail coach road ran through it and markets were held every Thursday, "...much frequented by Sligo merchants who purchase butter in firkins for exportation." Also yarn and pigs were widely traded. Six large fairs were held annually, plus the town had a constabulary police station and a dispensary.[12]

Lewis was also quite impressed by Frenchpark Demesne, the home of Lord Arthur French, the brother of Rev. John French, the McCormack's landlord. He described French's massive brick mansion, the rent office where he presided over local court sessions, and the finely wooded deer park. All in all, the Demesne covered some 1500 acres, and even included a Roman Catholic chapel which the family, who were Ascendancy

---

[11] Samuel Lewis, *A Topographical Dictionary of Ireland* (London: S. Lewis, 1837). http://www.libraryireland.com/topog/F/Frenchpark-Boyle-Roscommon.php (accessed 3 Jan, 2013).
[12] Ibid.

Protestants, had built for their tenants. One gets the impression from Lewis that Frenchpark was a town destined for a distinguished future.

When we arrived some 150 years later, that bright future seemed to have passed Frenchpark by. By American standards, the village is tiny, little more than a crossroads. We parked in what seemed to be the town center, though there was not much town in evidence. I walked into the post office, which doubled as the pub, and asked if any McCormacks still lived nearby. Of course having the family name wouldn't necessarily mean that we were related, especially nearly a century after my grandmother's departure for America, but it was a place to start. "Ah," replied the postmaster, "You'll be wanting J. P." He proceeded to give me detailed directions to J.P. McCormack's farm. "Go down this road until you get to the monument. Turn right and go to the pump near Lavin's Shop. Then go up the lane and it's the last house." We did as instructed, and, with some trepidation, I knocked on the door. I asked the woman who answered "Is this the McCormack house?" "Oh no," she answered, "It's the next place." Next place? I was confused because we seemed to be already at the end of the road, but there was indeed a faint track beyond, though I could see no house. We had come this far, and it seemed foolish to give up, so I drove on, hoping not to lose the rental car in a ditch or rut. Another house appeared ahead. I stopped in front and watched a balding, middle-aged farmer walking slowly toward us looking very curious. He was obviously thinking that we must be the most lost tourists in Ireland. "Are you J. P. McCormack?" I asked, "My name is Tom Callahan." He smiled and replied "Well, I had an Aunt Kate who married a Callahan from Cloonfad." I had come to the right place.

By good fortune I had found my father's first cousin, John Patrick, better known as J. P. McCormack, son of my grandmother's youngest brother Martin. Even better, he still lived at the original family farm, from which my grandmother and five of her siblings had left for America many decades earlier. He invited us in for tea and told us a bit about the

McCormacks in Ireland. There were, he said, nine children in my grandmother's generation – I would later discover that he was wrong about this – most of whom emigrated to America in the late-19th and early-20th centuries. He knew nothing of his American cousins save a couple of surnames, and it became clear that there had been no contact between the American and Irish branches of the family since the late 1940s. He rummaged around in a box and gave me a couple of photographs to bring home, including one of the original house which had since been demolished and the foundation turned into a pig sty. He said that he had two surviving sisters, one, a farmer's wife living locally and one a nurse in England. After a delightful hour or so, we exchanged addresses and Ellen and I headed back to Cashel. Over the next few years we exchanged annual Christmas cards with short notes included, but I made no attempt to dig much further into the family history. By the time I did, it was almost too late.

My father died in 1993, the last of his generation of the Callahan branch of the family. In December 2002, I got a short letter from Beatie Dowd, J.P.'s sister, informing me that J. P. had died of a massive heart attack in hospital over a year earlier. As Beatie put it, "He never spoke again."[13] I had dabbled a bit over the years looking for ancestors based on what J.P. had told me and on an intriguing letter I had found among my father's papers. The 1980 letter was from an attorney named William J. McCormack of West Orange, NJ concerning the disposal of a property in West Orange as part of the settlement of an estate. Why did my father have a copy? The letter named a number of McCormacks and McCormicks in New Jersey, some McLoughlins in Ireland and "Callahans in upper New York State."[14] So, it seemed that I must be related to these McCormacks and McLoughlins, and now I had some names and addresses. The early 1990s, of course, were the days before the Internet, and people were not so easy to find. I discovered that the addresses

[13] Beatie Dowd, letter to Thomas Callahan, 2 December 2002, collection of author.
[14] William J. McCormack, letter to Robert G. Beck, esq., 4 February 1980, collection of author.

were now useless and that William J. McCormack had been dead for a decade. I did, however, have his home address and phone number. Figuring I had nothing to lose, I called it and met Grace McCormack, William's daughter, who still lived in the family home. I had found my first American McCormack cousin. She was the granddaughter of Thomas McCormack, my grandmother's older brother, a West Orange policeman who had died in 1938. Grace's father was his only child, and Grace and her younger sister Jeanne were William's only children. We had a nice chat on the phone, and she told me there were other cousins in New Jersey as well. I promised myself to look further into the family history, and then completely ignored it until 2001.

In early January of that year I received an e-mail at my university from Tara McCabe, Grace's niece in Iowa. Tara was working on a McCormack genealogy, and Grace had mentioned my 1994 call. We each knew some things that the other did not, but neither of us was very certain of specifics beyond our immediate families. We exchanged information through the wonders of cyberspace, and I vowed once again, now that the search would be easier, to get down to business researching my family's history. I then ignored my pledge for nearly a decade.

A few years ago I began to teach our History Department's course on the History of Ireland. Many of the students who elected the course had Irish surnames, and would sometimes ask me about my own Irish roots. What did I really know? It was embarrassing. I knew that my grandmother had come from Ireland sometime before 1899 when she married Patrick Callahan in New Lebanon, NY. I knew this because I had photos of their 50th wedding anniversary in 1949 – in fact I am in one of the pictures, jauntily dressed for the occasion in a Roy Rogers cowboy suit. Also, I had inherited the steamer trunks in which they had brought all their worldly possessions to America, my grandmother's having her name stenciled on the end. I had my grandmother's passport listing her place of birth, and my grandfather's death certificate listing his. I knew I had cousins in Ireland and New Jersey, but I didn't know most of their names, who was still alive, or where they were. Overall, I had little more in 2009 than I had possessed thirty years earlier – except, finally, the will to use my historical training to find the history of the McCormacks here and in Ireland.

Chapter 2
Irish Roots

When the R. M. S. Campania sailed into New York harbor on April 17, 1897, Katie stared in awe at the great city spread out before her. She knew from her brothers' letters that New York was big, but she'd never seen anything like this before in her life! And that statue! It was just beautiful. Disembarking, she stepped in line at Ellis Island with hundreds of others waiting to be processed through Immigration. Finally, after questions about her age, origin, destination and whether she was just visiting or planned to stay, she passed the cursory physical examination and was admitted to the United States.

As she exited the Great Hall, now reunited with her steamer trunk, she saw Delia, her brother Patrick's wife, waiting for her, surrounded by three small children and holding an infant in her arms. They embraced, and the children, shy at first, crowded around their Aunt Katie. How is everyone? Delia hesitated, but finally told Katie that Patrick was gravely ill. He had something the doctors called Bright's Disease which was destroying his kidneys. He'd been barely able to work for weeks. Still, he was anxious to see his little sister again; she'd been only 10 when he left home.

They were soon off on the train for West Orange, New Jersey, where she'd also see John, Thomas and Michael again. Her brothers came over to Patrick's house when they finished work for the day and Katie brought them up to date on the folks back on the farm. She was away from home, but there were now more of them here than there!

Despite the doctor's best efforts, over the next few weeks Patrick weakened, and in just three months he was dead at age 30, leaving his young wife Delia, only 28 herself, to arrange for his wake and to care for their three small children and an infant.

Ireland at the time of Patrick's and Catherine's marriage had emerged from the chaos of The Famine as a very different country from the one that had had existed just a few decades earlier. The English had laid claim to the island in the 12th century on the basis that Pope Adrian IV had given it to them. Over the course of the next few centuries they had gradually turned this dubious claim into actual control of the country. Ireland became England's first colony, with its king recognized as the ruler of both lands. The Irish had their own parliament by the 15th century, but it could pass no acts without the express permission of the king. In the next century the relationship of the two countries became more complicated when England broke away from the Catholic Church and gradually became Protestant. This conversion had contributed to growing hostility to England from Europe's Catholic nations, in particular France and Spain. To a large degree this enmity was due to the usual rivalries among great powers, but the addition of religion into the mix had ominous consequences for Ireland.

The Irish remained steadfastly Catholic, and although they posed no serious threat to their powerful neighbor themselves, they could still be potentially dangerous. Ireland was seen as England's Achilles heel in that if an enemy like Spain or France were welcomed by the Irish, they could attack England more easily than across the Channel. So, in the 17th century England became much more aggressive in its suppression of the island. Irish persistence in clinging to Catholicism, an aborted rebellion in 1641 and their support for Charles I had led to Cromwell's bloody invasion in 1649 and the subsequent legislative onslaught in 1653. England confiscated over eleven million acres of land from Irish Catholics and banished tens of thousands of them to the west in the winter of 1653-54. This action is remembered by the Irish in the form of the famous phrase attributed to Cromwell that the Irish could go "to Hell or to Connacht."[1]

The restoration of the English monarchy in 1660 did not particularly help the Irish, even though Charles II was sympathetic to Catholicism and his brother James II was himself Catholic. In fact, when James was deposed in 1688 and was

---

[1] Though this phrase has been widely attributed to Cromwell for centuries, there is no definitive proof that he actually said it.

supported by most of Ireland, the English were determined to subdue the Catholic population once and for all. What followed were the infamous Penal Laws enacted by Ireland's Protestant parliament between 1695 and 1727. They were similar to anti-Catholic legislation in England, but there Catholics comprised only a small minority of the population while in Ireland they were the overwhelming majority. The purpose of the laws, simply put, was to deprive Irish Catholics of all political rights and as much land as possible. For example, Catholics could not buy land, take leases longer than 31 years, or inherit land from Protestants. Catholics had to will their property equally to all sons, so that the size of their holdings would become progressively smaller each generation. But, if one son converted to Protestantism, he was to get the entire inheritance. As a result, by 1774 Catholics owned a mere five per cent of the land in Ireland.[2]

By the late 18th Century many of the Penal Laws had fallen into disuse, as the English had, they thought, effectively subdued Catholic Ireland. But alarm was soon raised once again as the American Revolution stripped away most of Britain's North American colonies. What if England's failure abroad encouraged rebellion closer to home? The real panic struck with the French Revolution, beginning in 1789. Slogans like "Liberty, Equality, Fraternity" sounded good to many Irish, even to some stalwarts of the Protestant ruling class, who chafed under rule by the English Parliament. The Society of United Irishmen formed in 1791 to demand more freedom, and some sought out the military help of revolutionary France. The resulting failed 1798 rebellion, which actually saw a French army land in Ireland, though too little, too late, convinced the English government that Ireland had to be more tightly and completely controlled. So the British government now sought a permanent political union, like the annexation of Scotland a century earlier. Though reluctant at first to give up their independent parliament, enough of the Protestant gentry were convinced or bribed by English agents to

---

[2] Ranelagh, *Short History*, 71.

vote the Irish parliament out of existence in 1800. In 1801 Ireland was annexed to what was now called the United Kingdom of Great Britain and Ireland. The same wealthy Protestants would still represent the Irish population, but they would now sit in Westminster rather than Dublin, and comprise only a small portion of the British Parliament, where their influence would be scant.

The prospect of the Union had been made more palatable to wealthy Irish Catholics by Prime Minister Pitt's promise that union would be followed by Catholic electoral emancipation, giving them the right to participate in politics for the first time since 1691. This promise, however, proved hollow when George III adamantly refused to even consider the matter and Pitt's own party turned on him. Though Pitt had done the honorable thing by resigning, the fact still remained that Irish Catholics remained legally barred from sitting in Parliament. The subsequent struggle for Catholic emancipation brought politicians like Daniel O'Connell to prominence and finally resulted in victory in 1829. Though a significant step forward in integrating Catholics into Irish political life, emancipation also had unexpected negative consequences. Irish landowners, known since the 18th century as The Ascendancy, began to realize now that their Catholic tenants could vote, they might become valuable political assets as well as rent payers.

By this time, although the days of the harsh Penal Laws had passed, approximately 90% of Irish land was still in the hands of these 5000 Ascendancy landowners, many of whom desired a seat in Parliament in addition to being lords of their manors.[3] Irish landholding patterns were extremely complex before The Famine. Many in The Ascendancy rented land to prosperous tenant farmers who in turn split it into ever smaller plots to sub-let. There were often several layers of tenants of varying wealth, ranging from what were termed "strong farmers" who held over 30 acres, down to the extremely poor who might rent as little as a quarter of an acre. Small farms vastly outnumbered larger ones.

---

[3] Ibid, 101.

Over 90% of holdings in Connacht in 1841 were less than 15 acres.[4] Even such a small plot, if planted with potatoes, could feed a family. Simply put, many landowners encouraged repeated sub-division of their property to increase the number of potential, presumably loyal, voters at election time.

To marry and establish an independent household, a man had to hold land, rented or otherwise, and, with increasing subdivision, many new families came into being in the decades following emancipation. Ireland's population exploded in the first half of the 19th century, making the country ripe for the disaster brought on by the almost complete failure of the potato crop in the late 1840s. When The Famine ended, landholding patterns began to change. The Ascendancy still owned most it, but small holdings increasingly gave way to larger farms that could be more productive and profitable.

A comparison of The Famine's aftermath with that of the Black Death which had swept through much of Europe five hundred years earlier, killing millions and reducing the population by an estimated 30% to 40%, reveals a stark contrast. Ireland did not bear the brunt of this disease, but experiences in England can be instructive. As with the later Famine, the plague had swept away many of the poor, but entrenched, peasants, shattering centuries-old customs and providing landholders with opportunities for change. What came to be called enclosures eliminated much "common land" and age-old traditions of farming. The sudden drop in population actually worked to the peasants' advantage, making their wage labor more valuable since land still needed to be cultivated, while the potential labor force had contracted considerably. Peasants demanded lower rents and higher wages as the last vestiges of serfdom disappeared. Noble resistance to these demands led Parliament to pass the Statute of Laborers in 1351, fixing wages at their early 1330s level and forbidding laborers from refusing any offer of work at those wages.

---

[4] F. H. A. Aalen, *Man and the Landscape in Ireland* (London: Academic Press, 1978), 214.

Eventually, peasant resentment toward this law and other indignities forced upon them led to the dramatic but doomed English Peasants' Revolt of 1381. Still, economic conditions assured that English peasants emerged from the disaster of the plague generally better off than they had been.

In Ireland five hundred years later, however, the end of The Famine did little to invigorate Irish agriculture. There were now considerably fewer farmers and agricultural laborers, but this did not translate into prosperity for those who remained, particularly in hard-hit areas such as Connacht. The extensive shift from tillage to grazing meant that fewer laborers were needed, and the phasing out of holdings of less than five acres resulted in fewer sons being able to get a small portion of their family's holding so that they could marry and start their own families. More and more, farms were passed intact from generation to generation. This trend also deprived many Irish women of the opportunity to marry, plus prospective husbands who had to wait for their parents to die before inheriting land now were often much older than before. In addition, the advent of large-scale commercial farming in England, plus the growing ease and shrinking expense of transporting agricultural goods, put Irish farmers at a severe disadvantage. To make matters even worse, the industrial revolution in England and *laissez-faire* trade policies pursued by its government had destroyed most native industry in Ireland, except for the linen mills. Irish cities stagnated in the 19th century; with the exception of Dublin, most contracted in size. So excess rural men and women were faced with bleak prospects indeed. They could not migrate to growing factory towns such as those which absorbed English farm folk. They could stay home and single, working on their parents' and brothers' farms, competing for whatever seasonal work that might be available, or they could emigrate, an increasingly popular alternative. Even with the end of The Famine, wholesale emigration continued. Between 1856 and 1920, over 3.5 million emigrants abandoned their homeland in search of a brighter future.[5]

Beyond the general trends outlined above, scholars have fiercely debated the condition of Irish agriculture in the late-19th century.[6] Though recent historians using sophisticated statistical analyses have painted a much more nuanced portrait of landlord-tenant relations and agricultural trends than was generally accepted several decades ago, their conclusions still point to hard times for Irish farmers, especially in Connacht where the McCormack family originated. Though the crisis of The Famine had passed, as Barbara Solow argued in her 1971 study of the Irish land question: "[t]he fatal combination of dense population, small farms and no possibility of profitable tillage imprisoned Connacht and the Northwest in virtually a pre-famine mold."[7] The potato crop continued to be a staple for most small farmers, but was still extremely vulnerable as late as the 1880's before the adoption of an effective preventative spray called the Bordeaux mixture. Potato yields had been bad in 1860 and 1872, and harsh weather conditions in 1877 and 1879 had proven disastrous.[8] Plus, when cheap imported American grain could compensate for low local yields, Irish farmers could not even benefit from higher prices for their lower harvests because of supply and demand. Just about all Irish farm products were more cheaply obtained from America, Europe and elsewhere due to more efficient farming and inexpensive transport. Sharp price

---

[5] Miller, *Emigrants and Exiles*, 349.

[6] The state of Irish agriculture in the 19th century has attracted many scholars and much debate. See the earliest scholarly study, J. E. Pomfret, *The Struggle For Land in Ireland 1800-1923* (Princeton: Princeton University Press, 1930) and later writers who question some of his conclusions: W. E. Vaughn, *Landlords and Tenants in Mid-Victorian Ireland* (Oxford: Oxford University Press, 1994); B. Solow, *The Land Question in the Irish Economy 1870-1903* (Cambridge: Harvard University Press, 1971) and S. Clark, *Social Origins of the Irish Land War* (Princeton: Princeton University Press, 1979).

[7] Solow, *Land Question*, 111.

[8] Ibid., 112-122.

declines for Irish farm products sent both graziers and tillage farmers deeply into debt.[9]

The trend away from tillage toward grazing picked up speed after these later crop failures. In addition, there was increasing tension between tenants and landlords. The most dramatic result of tenant hardship in the late-19th century was the land war which pitted tenants against landlords over the so-called "three F's" – fixity of tenure, fair rents and free sale. Tenants demanded security on their holdings; landlords should not be able to evict a rent-paying tenant and replace him by someone who was willing to pay more. Rents should also be "fair," though what this meant could be variously interpreted. Finally, tenants should be able to sell the value of whatever improvements they had made to the land at their own expense. As it was, the law considered all improvements [e.g. new outbuildings, improved drainage and such] as belonging to the landlord. So, there was no real incentive for tenants to make any improvements which increased the value of the property for fear that the owner would then evict the current holder and bring in a new, higher paying tenant.

What the farmers wanted was for Ulster Custom, which already embodied these principles in the north, to be enshrined in law for the whole island. Rent strikes, boycotts and considerable violence broke out in the early 1880s as the Land League focused tenants' demands against the colonial rulers. While modern studies have shown that in fact the vast majority of landlords never evicted rent-paying tenants and that rents were not unduly high, Land League demands clearly touched a raw nerve among farmers. Even if most farmers were not actually exploited, the potential for exploitation existed. In 1876 a government survey of landowning showed that 110 men owned 20% of the country, and a further 1,878 held an additional 50%. So, fewer than 2000 landholders owned 70% of Ireland, while their three million tenants and laborers owned virtually no property at all.[10] This was clearly a potentially explosive issue

---

[9] Miller, *Emigrants and Exiles*, 388, 391.
[10] Ranelagh, *Short History*, 136.

which tested the English government's commitment to supporting The Ascendancy's rights as landowners as separate from their role as rulers.[11] The resulting Land Act of 1881 was largely a validation of Irish tenant demands. Government commissions reduced rents and offered low interest loans to enable farmers to purchase their holdings, and, although significant changes in ownership patterns were still in the future, it was already clear that well organized resistance would catch the attention of the ruling class.

English officials worried a great deal about Ireland in the late-19th century. In 1800 the upper class, which controlled Parliament, had seen incorporating Ireland into Great Britain as the first step toward a smooth integration of the two lands. Ireland on its own, or as a loosely controlled colony was dangerous, a potential back door to invade Britain. The same logic which led British rulers to tighten their grip on Ireland to prevent possible Spanish exploitation in the 16th Century, now renewed English fears in the face of the French Revolution and the Napoleonic empire. If a foreign enemy got a foothold in Ireland, England's defenses would be gravely endangered. Besides, the English reasoned, they could modernize and improve the backward Irish, bringing them the benefits of free trade and English culture. The fact that the vast majority of Ireland's population was Catholic was a worry, but not a major one. Several decades later, however, British frustration was growing. The Famine had clearly been a disaster, and the Irish were seen as ungrateful for the help they had been given. They stubbornly clung to old ways, and more and more Irish refused to accept the English view that they were better off than in 1800. The decades since 1800 had reinforced the English view of the Irish as a nation of backward lazy ingrates. The English Liberal party, led by William Gladstone in the late-19th century had made efforts to change this perception as well as to deal more fairly with the Irish. Gladstone's efforts on Ireland's behalf,

---

[11] Ibid.

however, did little to change this negative view. By the end of the century the Victorian ideal of "reforming" the Irish to act more English was commonly viewed as a hopeless cause. Consequently, much of England's Irish policy now hinged on placating Ireland's Catholic population to keep them from being attracted to increasingly radical nationalist sentiments.

Chapter 3
The Hunt Begins

Now that her husband was dead, Delia decided to take her children to Pittsfield, Massachusetts where most of her own family, the Callaghans, lived. They were from Cloonfad, near Frenchpark, and many had settled near the New York State border in the previous generation. Delia and Patrick McCormack had known each other back home, both of their families having attended the same small church in Tibohine. Though Patrick had brothers in New Jersey, the shock of his death made Delia want to be once again with her own kin, at least for a while. She asked Katie to come along and to help her with the children.

So Kate McCormack headed north where she would meet again Patrick Callaghan, Delia's younger brother. Kate and Pak, as he was called, had not seen each other for over two years, since Pak had come to America. Back home there would have been no chance that they would ever marry since he would not be inheriting the family farm or have money to purchase land of his own. Nor would Kate's family have provided her with a dowry. Pak and Kate had left Ireland precisely because they had no future there. But here in America you were on your own, free to remake yourself as you wished. In fact, both Pak and Kate had already taken advantage of this opportunity, shaving three years off their ages when questioned on their arrival at Ellis Island, believing that younger workers were more likely to be hired. You were also free in America to marry whom you wished. Pak still had no land, but he had a good steady job on the section crew of the Rutland Railroad just over the New York State border in Lebanon Springs. On September 3rd, 1899, Patrick Callahan, as he now spelled his last name, and Catherine McCormack married and moved into a small cottage rented from the Lebanon Mountain Shaker Community for $5.00 per month. Delia, and her children Thomas, Patrick, William and Mollie moved in with them.

My preparation to teach our Irish History course had familiarized me with the general themes of 19th century Ireland,

and I had explored them with my students over several semesters. But we had not conducted any in-depth studies of localities. What were conditions actually like in rural Roscommon and Frenchpark after The Famine? How had they affected my grandmother's family? My graduate school training in the late 1960s had come at the beginning of the "history from the bottom up," or social history movement which rebelled against examining the past from the vantage point of societies' elites. Its advocates extolled the rewards of examining the bottom of society where the vast majority had lived rather than the top where the "ruling classes" prevailed. It is undoubtedly a useful approach to history which enriches our understanding of the past, but one fraught with grave limitations.

Whatever else one might think about the elites and their role in shaping history, you had to admit that they usually left a clear trail of their activities. Letters, memoirs, and documents of all kinds laid out the thoughts and actions of the upper classes. Kings, presidents, prime ministers and generals left more grist for the historian's mill than did peasants, workers and privates. Just ask most people about their great-grandparents. Unless they were rich and/or politically important, you'll be lucky to even learn their names. Consequently, many practitioners of the new approach relied heavily on statistical studies and other investigative tools which could reveal a great deal about the common people in the aggregate even if they did not know much about particular men and women. Still, the innovative new research paths led to a much expanded understanding of the "common people" in the past – common people such as the McCormacks. First I would find as much specific information as possible about the family, then investigate how these facts fit into the general trends of emigration and life in Ireland.

Now that I had the will, I had to find a way to recover the family's history on a trail that had long gone cold. My first thought was to call Grace McCormack again. I had no idea how old she or her sister were, but suspected that they were probably in their 70s since their grandfather was older than my grandmother, plus my father had been 38 when I was born. So I hoped that she was still living sixteen years after I had last spoken to her. I was rewarded with a message from AT&T that "This number is no longer in service." I assumed the worst, not knowing that the area code had merely changed and that Grace was still alive and well. I next turned to finding Grace's niece Tara, who had lived in Davenport, Iowa in 2001. Her e-mail address no longer worked, but Internet phone searches now made it easier to find people. How many Tara McCabes could there be in Davenport? Fortunately, there was only one. She remembered me and told me the wonderful news that not only was Grace still with us, but also that Tara's mother, Jeanne Lechner, was not only alive, but also used e-mail. Things were looking up on this side of the Atlantic.

But, what of Ireland? Was Beatie Dowd still living? I had not had a Christmas card from her in five years, plus I knew that she was from my father's generation and would be quite elderly. Not knowing what else to do, I sent her a letter at the last address I had. For those unfamiliar with Irish rural mailing addresses, they seem very vague, no house numbers, no street addresses, no postal codes. I hoped that the mail, even if Beatie had passed on, would be delivered to someone in her family who might be interested enough to contact me. I was excited a few weeks later to find an e-mail in my in-box from Beatie's youngest daughter, Catherine Carr. She wrote that her mother had indeed died, but she would be happy to help, as would her siblings, most of whom lived locally. In fact, her brother James had inherited the McCormack family homestead when J. P. died. She also informed me that J.P.'s and Beatie's oldest sister, Mai Robinson, nearly 90, was living in England. So, as 2010 began, I had reasonable hopes of success.

The Emigrants

I began my research with the American branch of the McCormacks. My own first cousins, the two that I could locate, knew little about their grandmother's family, but Grace and

Jeanne got me started in the right direction. They are the grandchildren of Thomas McCormack of West Orange, NJ, one of my grandmother's elder brothers. Thomas had come to America in 1892 and like his elder brother Patrick, worked at first as a gardener for local families. He later became a coachman, then a policeman in West Orange, and died in his late 60s in 1938. Jeanne heard that her grandfather was one of twelve children, whereas J. P. in Ireland told me nine. Subsequent research would prove Jeanne correct. Neither Jeanne nor her sister Grace had ever heard of the Callahans before I contacted them. Nor did they know much in detail about their McCormack aunts, uncles and cousins. Jeanne warned me that my search would be complicated. Some of the McCormacks used the spelling McCormick, plus an inordinate number of them were named William.

Jeanne's father was William J., plus there was also a William A. and William P. in the same generation in New Jersey. This plethora of Williams came to be a running joke among the cousins as my research progressed, as it was revealed that almost every McCormack who had male children named one of them William. In fact, I discovered early on that my own Uncle John Callahan, my father's brother, was actually named William John. No one can account for the name's popularity. Neither Grace nor Jeanne had any idea what had become of their father's cousins William A. and William P., except that they had both sired sons named, of course, William. There had also been an "Auntie Bea" Daniels somewhere in New Jersey who was my grandmother's younger sister. There was also an "Uncle Michael," who may or may not have been another of the twelve [nine?] siblings. At Jeanne's suggestion, I checked a number of on-line people finders over the next couple of weeks, only to discover that the name William McCormack was stunningly popular even beyond our own family. It was time for some professional help, so I bought a subscription to *Ancestry.com*, which draws upon the staggeringly huge data base of public and private genealogical records maintained by the Church of Latter Day Saints.

Ancestry.com provides access to vital statistics, census records, and a myriad other sources world-wide. It would have been nearly impossible to pursue this project without it, but there are limits to its use. For example, although all extant United States census records are on-line and searchable, the government's most recent release is the 1940 census. There is a 72-year blackout period to protect the privacy of living citizens. Also, most states have not released vital statistics records on-line, so finding birth, death and marriage information requires a trip to the state's archives. In the case of New Jersey, where most of the American McCormack records are stored, this is not a particular problem for me since I live less than 10 miles away, plus, even better, my wife Ellen works there. There are, however, further restrictions. Privacy laws in New Jersey restrict access to any records after 1940 and do not allow researchers to browse through this material, which is essential when one does not know exact dates, etc., of births, deaths and marriages. Still, despite such limitations, the convenience and access provided by *Ancestry.com* is well worth it. A valuable bonus to their service is that many international records are available on-line as well.

Now I pursued a two-pronged research plan: I continued looking for McCormack cousins while I searched the public records for clues. I began my on-line search with what I knew best, the Callahan family from upstate New York. Since I knew much about them already, I should be able to recognize which *Ancestry* results were relevant, and learn to navigate their system more easily and efficiently.

--

I found that the more you already knew, the easier it was to get good results from *Ancestry*. Using the "Advanced Search" option where one supplies such information as spouse's name, I quickly found my grandparents in the available United States census records. Each census asked slightly different questions, so, taken together, much is revealed. In 1930, for example, the government not only asked for your vital statistics facts on birth, marriage, citizenship, children and such, but also if you owned a radio. They did. Ten years earlier showed that eight of their nine children had been born, and their names and ages were listed. Going back to 1900, the earliest relevant census for my grandparents who had married in 1899, I discovered that they had five "boarders," Delia McCormack, a widow, and her four young children.[1] Who was she? With the McCormack last name, they must be relatives, but I had no idea what the relationship was. I figured that Delia was an uncommon name, perhaps making it easy to find her and her children in later census surveys.

I knew from the 1910 census records from Lebanon Springs, NY where my grandparents lived, that the boarders were no longer there, but where had they gone? I searched the 1910 census using Delia's name, age and children's names and found her in West Orange, NJ.[2] She and her three surviving children lived on Llewellyn Avenue, and a perusal of her neighbors revealed another McCormack family – actually a McCormick family, but Jeanne had forewarned me that this anomaly would appear. So, John McCormick was probably Delia's brother-in-law, but who was Delia's husband? The 1900 census had given Delia's children's names and ages and had stated that they had been born in New Jersey. I asked my wife to look for their birth records, which she easily found. Delia's husband had been named Patrick. I knew he was dead by 1900, so we looked for his death certificate. Another success – Patrick had died in August 1897 at age 30 of Bright's Disease, which I later learned was an acute kidney ailment.[3] Riding a wave of investigative success, we next searched for Delia and Patrick's marriage certificate and found that they had been married in January 1892, and that one of the witnesses was Thomas McCormack, Grace and Jeanne's

---

[1] US Department of the Interior, Census Office, Twelfth Census, 1900, New Lebanon Town, Columbia County, New York, Enumeration District 26, Sheet 16 A and B, s.v, "McCormick, Delia."

[2] Ibid., Thirteenth Census, 1910, West Orange, Ward 3, Essex County, New Jersey, Enumeration District 226, Sheet 1A, s.v." McCormick, Delia."

[3] New Jersey State Archives, Department of Health, Bureau of Vital Statistics, Death Certificates and Indexes, 1878-1946, Essex County M-41.

grandfather.[4] What really caught my eye, however, was Delia's maiden name: Callaghan. Could she have been my grandfather's sister? Her parents, Patrick and Madge, were the same as his, so yes, she was. Delia and her children were obviously lodging with her brother and sister-in-law. This was amazing; I was related by blood to both Delia and Patrick. My grandparents had not been the first to unite the Callaghan and McCormack families.

As tempting as it was to pursue both the Callahan and McCormack ancestors, I resolved to keep my focus on my grandmother's family. At this point I knew that Kate had at least three brothers living in West Orange, plus a possible fourth, Michael. Soon I found John McCormack's marriage record from 1888, listing Patrick as a witness.[5] Census records had Patrick, John and Thomas arriving from Ireland between 1886 and 1893; Kate had arrived in 1897. Michael remained a mystery, as there were a number of Michael McCormacks in the census records; without knowing more, I would have great difficulty sorting them out. At this point I had a stroke of extraordinary good luck. Jeanne Lechner and I had been discussing how to find various other cousins including Delia's descendants, but without a great deal of progress. She had heard of "Aunt Bea," but had never met her. She knew that William A. McCormack, who was her godfather and possibly Delia's son, had had two children. She remembered the girl's name, Jeanne, for obvious reasons, but could not remember the son. Neither she nor Grace had any idea where either of them might be. She did, however, have another clue. One of Jeanne Lechner's high school classmates in 1951 was Ann Connors, who had married into another branch of the family who spelled their names McCormick. She had re-married at some point, but her name and address were in Jeanne's 55th high school reunion souvenir booklet. I do not like to call people "cold" and possibly have my intentions misunderstood, so I wrote Ann, now Krenkowitz, a letter of inquiry on university stationery to show that I was an actual college professor, in case

---

[4] Ibid., Marriage Certificates and Indexes, 1878-1940, Patrick McCormack/Delia Callaghan, Essex County, M-59.
[5] Ibid., John McCormack/Ann Morrisroe, 6 December, 1888, Essex County, M-8.

that might matter. It was now early February, and Jeanne wished me good luck and headed for Florida for a few weeks.

A few days later I received a call from Ann Krenkowitz. She wished me well in my search, but said that she really didn't remember much about her first husband's family, especially since he had died over 40 years earlier. Ann told me, however, that she did know someone who knew a lot about the McCormicks, Patricia McCormick Davis, daughter of another of the Williams, who lives in Bay Head, NJ. Ann said that she would contact Patricia to be sure that it was alright to give me her phone number. Number soon in hand, I gave Patty a call. We hit it off immediately and talked for over an hour. She is the daughter of William P. McCormick and the granddaughter of John, who lived on Llewellyn Avenue next to Delia. In fact, Patty was brought up in John's house and lived there with her husband before moving to Bay Head in the mid-1990s. My good fortune was two-fold: Patty was extremely interested in my project, and also knows more about the American branch of the family than anyone else. In addition, she has a marvelous collection of old family photos which she has generously shared. With Patty's help I began to make rapid progress. There were still plenty of gaps and mysteries, but the basic picture of the American McCormacks – and McCormicks – was becoming clear.

This was an exciting time, both professionally and personally. On one level I was now convinced that I could actually complete this project successfully; there was going to be enough evidence to reconstruct a history of the McCormacks. While, except for Patty, most of the cousins knew little outside of their own branch of the family, collectively we knew a great deal. Before long I would have, I then thought, the names of all of my grandmother's siblings, and could begin to discover what became of them, both here and in Ireland. On another, more personal, level, I, an only child with scant contact with my Callahan cousins, now had a large family! Over the next few months I would meet nearly twenty of them.

While I searched for records of the McCormacks in America I also began arranging a trip to Ireland. Some twenty years earlier my last visit had been a vacation; meeting J. P. had largely been luck. Now I planned to do some research at the National Archives and National Library and to travel once more to Frenchpark to meet and interview descendants of family members who had remained at home.

Before that trip, however, I had plenty of work to do. I wanted to spend my time in Ireland as productively as possible, and to accomplish that I first needed to make sense of how the various relatives and family branches fit together. Through a rapid series of e-mail exchanges with Patty Davis I established that my grandmother had four older brothers and a younger sister who lived in New Jersey, most of them in or near West Orange. The eldest, John, was Patty's grandfather. I would later learn that he had married Anne Morrisroe, a young woman he had known in Ireland, in 1888, and they had seven children between 1890 and 1904. Next in age was Patrick, who had married Delia Callaghan in 1893 and died in 1897. They had four children. Thomas, Grace and Jeanne's grandfather, and his wife Annie Hoare married in 1900 and had one child.[6] Michael, who Patty helped me sort out from the dozens of possibilities on *Ancestry.com*, had three children. When he first appeared in the census records he was already a widower, so I did not yet know anything about his date of marriage or his wife, except that she was dead by 1920. My grandmother Catherine was the next eldest, and I knew a great deal about her and her family. She and Patrick had produced nine children between 1900 and 1921. Her younger sister Bea, Beatrice Daniels, and her husband Ernest had three children, though I did not yet know about the third. So, the six McCormack immigrant siblings in America had added twenty-seven new citizens to the United States. I felt pretty good about my progress to this point, especially considering that I did not even know these people's names a few months earlier.

---

[6] Ibid., Thomas McCormack/Anna Hoare, 25 April 1900, Essex County, M-167.

Patty then informed me that another branch of the McCormacks also lived in New Jersey, the McLoughlins. Paddy [Patrick] McLoughlin, the youngest son of Margaret McCormack, the eleventh and last of my grandmother's siblings, had emigrated to the United States after World War II, raised a family and owned a bar in West Orange until his death in 2008. He had later been followed by his younger sister, Maureen, who had also established her family here. Other McLoughlin siblings had stayed in Ireland or moved to England. Of particular interest was the fact that two of Paddy's sisters, now quite elderly, were still living, Sister Joseph, a retired nun in Belfast and Katie, a widow in England. Perhaps they would be able to help me with some first-hand information from the early 20th century. I soon discovered that Katie was in very poor health, and I was not able to contact her before her death in 2010. Sister Joseph, however, has provided some very useful information from the early 20th century.

By the beginning of spring 2010 the Irish trip was set. Ellen and I would divide our time between the west where my grandmother and her siblings had been born and where most of the descendants of those who remained still lived, and Dublin where I could pursue research at the National Archives and National Library. By a lucky coincidence, six of Martin McCormack's eight grandchildren were gathering in Boyle for a family first communion during our stay. So, I would get to meet them and discuss family history. I bought a new laptop and loaded it with photos and documents to show my cousins. I also hoped to find photos and letters there to scan and add to the materials I already had.

We arrived in Boyle, some seven miles north of Frenchpark, and soon met the first of my Irish cousins, Catherine Carr, J.P. McCormack's youngest niece. She and her husband Andrew gave us a general overview of the area and pointed us in the right directions to visit various cemeteries to find ancestral graves. They apologized for not being able to guide us personally, but they had to arrange for the first communion party for their son Enda a few days hence. So, we were on our own – but with good directions. Catherine also said that it would not be possible to go to the homestead, because the road had deteriorated considerably since J.P.'s death a decade earlier. His house was unoccupied, and, although the farm was still maintained by her brothers, John and James Dowd, it was quite isolated. Had we been able to stay in the area longer, John could have given us a tour, but we had to be off to Dublin the day after the family communion party.

The next morning we set out on what we named the "Cemetery Tour." There were four on our list, and we found them all easily. The most important one for my research was the "old" Tibohine cemetery, located right next to the Tibohine chapel a few miles outside of Frenchpark. Unfortunately, the graveyard is largely a mass of tumbled or lichen-encrusted stones, most nearly impossible to read. We had no idea where the family graves might be, nor at that time, exactly who was buried there. Plus, the morning was wet, the grass was high and we were too easily discouraged. Finding no ancestors at all, we moved on to other, newer, cemeteries which were better maintained. Finding some modest success in gathering birth and death dates, we finished the day quite satisfied, though we knew that at some point on a future trip we would need to revisit Tibohine.

Tibohine would later prove to be more important and more interesting than we realized that wet May morning. Church marriage and baptismal records indicated that the McCormack's parish church was in Ballinameen, on the other side of Frenchpark, but I soon discovered that the family had actually attended church in Tibohine, which was much closer and more convenient for them. The area is still remarkably rural, as it was when Samuel Lewis described in 1837. Although he generally tried to write nice things about the places he visited, he described Tibohine, also called Taugboyne, as "[consisting] for the most part of isolated hills and ridges, bounded by bogs, forming altogether a wild tract, one-half bog and the other inferior land, under an unimproved system of agriculture."[7]

On subsequent days we visited the small church in Ballinameen where my grandmother's parents had married in 1861 and hunted down in Callow some McLoughlin cousins. Tom McLoughlin, grandson of the youngest of my grandmother's siblings, and his wife Ann were very gracious and had some splendid family photos to share. Then it was time for Enda's first communion and the family party. The party, at Catherine and Andrew's house outside of Boyle, was delightful. We met all of Catherine's siblings, the children of Beatie McCormack Dowd. Catherine's brother John, the eldest, greeted us with a question: "How long have you been home?" I was surprised at first, but we were indeed, in a way, Americans coming "home" to Ireland, and we were warmly welcomed as returning family members. As a fitting confirmation gift, we gave Enda a small brass cross that my grandmother had brought with her from Ireland over a century earlier.

Here we were, in the village where the McCormack family began and grew. In 1886 the twelfth and youngest child, Margaret, was born and the eldest, John, departed for America. It was the last year that Patrick, Catherine and their whole family were together.

Although Ireland was not hemorrhaging people in the late 19th century as it had during the Famine years, the flow was still very strong. Studies of Irish census figures show that around a quarter of those aged 5 to 24 "disappeared" from the population each decade before the next census was compiled. The population, which stood at 5.8 million in 1861 had declined to 4.3 million by 1926.[8] In fact, Ireland's population continued to decline until the latter half of the 20th Century.[9] During the Famine period, many

---

[7] Lewis, *Topographical Dictionary*. http://www.libraryireland.com/topog/T/Taugh-boyne-Boyle-Roscommon.php (accessed 18 February 2013).

[8] Fitzpatrick, "Emigration," 607; Miller, *Emigrants and Exiles*, 346.

[9] For in-depth accounts of Irish emigration in this period see G. Moran, *Sending Out Ireland's Poor* (Dublin: Four Courts Press, 2004), A. Schrier, *Ireland and the*

whole families had fled Ireland either willingly or by eviction, but the character of later emigration was quite different. Most emigrants now were single young adults traveling on their own. Also, a large proportion of them were female, an unusual phenomenon not seen in other large-scale European migrations. Remarkably, between 1893 and 1904 women consistently outnumbered males.[10] The vast majority of men classified themselves as "laborers" and women as "servants" on ship manifests, though many were actually farmers and women without any employment goals. By the hundreds of thousands they poured out of Queenstown, now the most popular port of embarkation rather than Liverpool, over 80% of them headed to the United States.[11]

Scholars often use a "push-pull" analogy to explain the causes of Irish emigration. In the Famine years, starvation, disease and desperate landlords had "pushed" the poor out, many against their will, turning them into exiles. Turned out of their homes and run off their holdings, or simply fleeing impending disaster, waves of poor, often ill, emigrants embarked on long perilous voyages on decrepit, leaky "coffin ships." Many died at sea, many others, ill and destitute, clogged the ports of Canada and America. As many as 30% of those who emigrated at this time died en route or soon after their arrival.[12] Later in the century, however, most emigrants were "pulled" out of Ireland by the prospect of a better life elsewhere. Those who left and found success abroad often advised or aided others to follow, a phenomenon known as chain emigration.[13] New arrivals encouraged their families and friends with words like "Dear friend, I mean to let you know that I can sit at a table as good as the best man in Belmullet. Thank God that I left that miserable

American Emigration 1850-1900 (Minneapolis: University of Minnesota Press, 1958); Miller, *Emigrants and Exiles.*

[10] Fitzpatrick, "Emigration," 612.

[11] Ibid., 608.

[12] Miller, *Emigrants and Exiles*, 292.

[13] Moran, *Ireland's Poor*, 64.

place."[14] This is not to deny that many poor, without much hope of employment or marriage at home, felt that they had to leave, but most of those who boarded ships at Queenstown between the 1860's and early 1900s left Ireland in a much more optimistic mood than their countrymen had done a generation earlier. Travel by modern steamship took little more than a week, and although steerage was never comfortable, passengers were not there for very long.

As in the Famine years, the highest rate of emigration came from Connacht, the Irish province with the most grinding poverty. They were forced out by an insidious combination of poor harvests, evictions and collapsing farm prices.[15] Agriculture throughout Ireland faced hard times, but the situation in the west was the worst. Infertile ground hastened conversion from tillage to pasture, and increasingly farmers in western counties like Roscommon came to rely on cattle for their livelihood. Yet the same steam technology that enabled emigrants to travel to America in about a week also ferried American farm products, including cattle from the mid-west, in the other direction. In the prevailing free market economy of Great Britain, Irish exports struggled to compete. Only with flax, and hence linen, was there much success. The situation became so serious that even the British government, notoriously reluctant to pour money into Ireland, established the Congested Districts Board in 1891, to encourage assisted emigration by the poorest of the poor.

There was some ebb and flow over the years in the pace of emigration due to relative economic conditions in Ireland and the United States, but the overall trend was up. Between The Famine and the end of the century, Ireland's population was cut in half.[16] The changes in international trade patterns which had taken hold by the 1880s had a profound effect on this emigration. Whereas in 1877, the last year of Irish agricultural prosperity, when fewer than 14,000 left for America, by 1883 the number had risen to 83,000 and remained high for the rest of the century.

---

[14] Ibid., 208.
[15] K. Kenny, *The American Irish* (London: Longman, 2000), 132.
[16] Ibid., 133.

Nearly a half million emigrated in the 1890s alone.[17] Investigation of Irish immigration into the United States reveals the startling fact that in 1900 the five million first and second generation Irish in America surpassed the entire population of Ireland by more than a half million.[18] In addition, the dangers of an ocean voyage had all but disappeared. With the new steamships, mortality rates had fallen to less than 1%, plus fierce competition among shipping companies had reduced the steerage fare to $8.75 by 1894, the equivalent of about one week's wages for an unskilled worker in the United States.[19] Relatives in the United States were sending home millions in remittances, much of which came in the form of pre-paid tickets to bring more of their families out. An estimate by Arnold Schrier puts the total of money orders alone from the United States to the United Kingdom, most of which went to Ireland, between 1872 and 1900 at nearly $96,000,000.[20] The results were dramatic. Looking at American and Irish census records, one can see that often whole neighborhoods were relocated across the Atlantic.

Many Irish were profoundly concerned about this persistent pattern of wholesale emigration. Essayists, editors and church officials bemoaned the trend and asked rhetorically why so many were leaving. Was it the lure of America? -- the aggressive sales campaigns of steamship companies and their agents? -- the lack of a promising future at home? They knew, of course, that the answer was "yes" to all of the above. However understandable the causes might be, however, most who wrote about emigration were against it. Newspapers predicted a bleak future for Ireland if emigration continued unabated. The country was losing its "youth and strength," its "bone and sinew," its "hope for the future."[21] As the young increasingly scrambled out of the country, Ireland was destined to become merely "one vast

---

[17] Miller, *Emigrants and Exiles*, 347.
[18] Kenny, *American Irish*, 131.
[19] Ibid, 140; Miller, *Emigrants and Exiles*, 355.
[20] Schrier, *Ireland*, 168.
[21] Ibid., 49.

sheepwalk and pasture."[22] For their part, the Catholic clergy worried mainly about the souls of those leaving. The United States in the 19th century was predominantly Protestant with few Catholic priests; who would minister to the emigrants' faith? Nationalists were particularly upset because they pinned their hopes on young, educated Irishmen and women to throw off the yoke of British rule. Their opposition to emigration became particularly virulent after the end of World War I when emigration once again picked up speed after the scourge of submarine warfare had been swept from the Atlantic. During the Anglo-Irish War in 1920, for example, the Republic's minister for defense declared that "...the young men of Ireland must stand fast. To leave their country at this supreme crisis would be nothing less than base desertion in the face of the enemy."[23]

All of these warnings and dire predictions had little effect in stemming the tide of emigration. Young Irish left the island in their millions, headed for what they hoped to be, and believed would be, a better life. They joined their brothers and sisters in America, wrote letters and sent money to their families at home. As families gathered to bid their loved ones a tearful farewell, "...port cities resembled cemeteries on a funeral day."[24] Those who were Irish when they embarked in Queenstown, became Irish-Americans in New York and Boston, and, within a generation or two, simply Americans. How were their lives changed? Were their expectations realized? What became of those they left behind?

---

[22] Ibid.

[23] Fitzpatrick, "Emigration," 632.

[24] L. McCaffrey, *The Irish Diaspora in America* (Bloomington: Indiana University Press, 1976), 72.

Chapter 4
Going Home

After eighteen years of marriage and seven children, Kate and Pak decided that it was time to move to a bigger house. Pak was now foreman of the section crew on the Rutland railroad, so he arranged for an empty boxcar to be parked on a siding 100 yards or so behind their cottage. Everyone pitched in; Mary and Madeline helped Kate pack up the clothes, pots, pans and linens while Auggie, John, Tom and even little Andy helped father carry the furniture. Robert was still too young to help, so his task was to stay out of the way. When the boxcar was loaded, it was coupled to the next train headed south to Chatham, and the whole family piled on. Pak's sister, Mary Griffin, and her husband Thomas moved into their vacated cottage. In Chatham the process was reversed and the family carried their worldly possessions to their rented apartment not 50 feet from the tracks. Compared to Lebanon Springs, the village of Chatham was a metropolis, nearly 3000 people and a dozen or more shops. The Callahans had definitely "arrived!"

Our sojourn in Roscommon had been rewarding. We met several family members and found a few photos that I scanned into my laptop. I left, however, somewhat disappointed. I had hoped to see some local parish records of births and deaths, but discovered that a fire had destroyed everything before 1900. Fortunately, they had been microfilmed, so I could see them later in Dublin. I had not gotten back to the family homestead, nor had I been able to find any McCormacks in the old Tibohine graveyard. In addition, there did not seem to be much in the way of family personal records, photographs or artifacts. The grand total for letters was two: one from America to Martin and his wife and one which I already had from them to my grandmother. These both dated from the late 1940s; I was surprised that there was nothing earlier. Overall, it was clear that the American cousins knew more about the Irish side of the family than they knew about us. When I remarked on this to

Patty Davis she said wisely "Maybe they are not interested in where they came from because they never left."

In Dublin I did research at the National Archives, National Library and the General Register office. At the National Library I found the marriage and baptism records for the parish of Ballinameen, where Patrick McCormack and Catherine Keenan had married and had their children baptized.[1] The microfilmed marriage records were virtually indecipherable due to the poor condition of the material, but the baptism records were in decent shape. The only problem was that they ended in 1880, thereby missing the last three McCormack children. Since I already had the approximate birthdates for most of the siblings, finding them was not difficult, though a quirk of the records was that the names were recorded in Latin. Thus John was recorded as "Johannes" and James "Jacobus" and so on. I would have to look elsewhere to find the last three, Martin, Beatrice and Margaret.

There was still the question of how many children there had actually been. The Irish cousins had heard that there were nine; Jeanne and Grace were told that there were twelve, and Patty's father had said thirteen. At the moment we had ten. So I figured as long as I had the records in front of me I'd check to see if there might be others. Catherine had borne children approximately every two years, but there were some gaps where unknown, perhaps stillborn children might have been. Had they lived long enough to be baptized, they should be here. There was one particularly suspiciously long gap between the birth of my grandmother in 1876 and her brother Martin in 1882. Cranking the microfilm reader through those months I discovered McCormack number eleven, Thadeus, born in 1879. His name seemed odd to me; what would he have actually been called once the Latin form of his name had been abandoned? A genealogist at the National Archives speculated that he would probably have been called Thady or Timothy. I had never heard of him, nor, as it turned out, had anyone else in the family. He

---

[1] Ballinameen Parish Marriages and Baptisms, 1859-1880, LDS Film 0989738, Batches C7011661, M701931.

probably died very young, though his death record has yet to be found. 1879 was a particularly difficult year for farmers in Roscommon, with conditions not much better than in the Famine years. Perhaps young Thadeus perished as a result.

Now we had identified eleven McCormack siblings; were there others? There was yet another anomaly in the birth records. The second son, Patrick, had been baptized in March 1864, but on his American marriage and death certificates his birth was listed as 1866. That discrepancy in itself was not a real concern, as most of the siblings who emigrated to the United States gave conflicting birthdates on various records. The problem was that a search of the LDS database for Irish birth records revealed two Patrick McCormacks born in Frenchpark in the 1860s, one in 1864 and the other in 1866. Were these two different people? The Ballinameen baptism records had a Patrick McCormack in 1866, but he had different parents, which seemed to clear up the confusion: yes there were two Patricks, but not in the same family. But – the LDS source also indicated a separate civil birth record for a Patrick with the right parents. On my return to the United States I ordered this microfilm and discovered that there were indeed *two* Patrick McCormacks born to Catherine Keenan McCormack and her husband, one in 1864 and the other in 1866.[2] Apparently the original Patrick died soon after his baptism, or at least before Catherine's next child was born two years later. Since Patrick was an important patrilineal name, they used it again. So the Patrick who emigrated to America and married Delia Callaghan was the second of that name, and we now had twelve siblings.

Discovering this second Patrick was still a ways off when we were in Dublin, but there was yet one more surprise in store. Ellen and I went to the General Register Office to look for civil birth and death certificates. These records had to be searched "the old-fashioned way," looking through annual indices and then requesting individual records to be photocopied by the staff. Potential problems abound. First, Irish records are not

---

[2] Ibid., Film 101083, Batch C701224.

complete; the Anglo-Irish war and subsequent civil war in the 1920's saw the wholesale destruction of many records. In addition, parents and families were themselves required to report births and deaths, which usually took place at home; in many cases no reports were ever made. We also discovered, not surprisingly, that McCormack and its variations like McCormick or M'cormack, was a very common surname, and one can hardly imagine how many Patricks, Johns or Catherines there are. Each requested search would cost four Euros, regardless of whether you found the right person.

I was particularly interested in finding the birth record for Beatrice McCormack, my grandmother's younger sister, born after the end date of the baptismal records. This was because of a mysterious Delia McCormack who appeared with the family on the 1901 census. Who was she? There were no gaps in the known birthdates to allow for yet another child. Perhaps she was a niece. The full census was released the week after we left, but there was already a partial record compiled by a Roscommon genealogist which had yielded Delia's name. The genealogist on duty at the National Archives told us that the names Delia and Beatrice were virtually interchangeable in Ireland, so finding Bea's birth record might clear this mystery up. Unfortunately, there were no Beatrice or Delia McCormacks from the right place or time in the index to the records. There was, however, a Bridget McCormack born in Frenchpark in the right year. So I gambled 4 Euros and got the record. On the 9th of October, 1883, Bridget McCormack was born to Patrick and Catherine Keenan McCormack of Slieveroe townland in Frenchpark.[3] What? Bridget, Delia and Beatrice were the **same** person! This was further confirmed in a few days when the full 1901 Irish census listed Delia McCormack, age 17, as "farmer's daughter."[4] My American cousins who had known "Auntie Bea" were stunned, except for Grace, who said she knew it all along. Grace's

---

[3] Ireland, General Register Office, Birth Records, Roscommon, Castlerea, Frenchpark, no. 89: Bridget McCormack, 9 October, 1883.

[4] National Archives of Ireland, 1901 Census, Roscommon/Frenchpark/Slieveroe, House #6: Delia McCormack, farmer's daughter.

grandfather's 1938 obituary stated that he was survived by, among others, "Mrs. Bridget Daniels of Newark." Bridget had come to the United States by 1903 and changed her name. "Nobody wanted to be Bridget in those days," Grace explained, as it was the common nickname for an Irish maid. Ironically, Bea began her life in the United States as an Irish maid.

The Register Office yielded one further valuable piece of information. No one now knew when the parents, Catherine and Patrick had died. I knew that Patrick was dead by 1901 because Catherine is listed in that census as a widow, and that he had been alive at least until 1885 because the last child, Margaret, had been born in 1886. I could find neither his birth or death date. Catherine appears in the 1911 census at age 69, putting her birth around 1842. A painstaking search of the death indices after 1911 offered up another 4-Euro gamble. It rewarded me with her death certificate showing that she had died in 1915 at age 73. Her youngest son, Martin, who inherited the farm, reported her death.[5]

Returning home, I needed to take stock of what I had learned and devise a system of arranging family facts and figures. First, I made a file box where everyone in my grandmother's and father's generations got their own folder to hold whatever information I gathered about them. Next, I compiled a useful document called "McCormack Vital Statistics" which sorted the McCormacks into their individual branches and listed everyone's birth, marriage and death dates. This made it much easier to keep track of who was who, who their parents, siblings and children were, and how the generations fit together. I would add pertinent dates whenever I found them. The list was also a stark reminder of what I actually knew about my ancestors and how much information I still needed to uncover. Later I added occupations for everyone as I learned them from census lists or cousins' memories. This second document, termed "McCormack

---

[5] General Register Office, Roscommon, Castlerea, Frenchpark, Death Records, 2 July 1915, Record 04460389, p. 79.

Family Occupations," vividly showed how the emigrant siblings and their children branched out into dozens of occupations, while those who remained in Ireland continued, for the most part, more traditional lives. My next goal was to learn all that I could about the emigrant generation's lives in America.

Six McCormack siblings left Ireland and settled in the United States between 1886 and 1903. When I began my current research, the only one I knew much about beyond their name and, for some, their occupation or other random facts was my grandmother, Catherine McCormack. She had been born in Frenchpark, County Roscommon, on 11 December, 1876, though she later claimed Christmas eve, 1879, and had died on 28 December, 1952. I did not yet know when she had arrived in the United States, though I knew she had been married here in 1899, because I had photos of her 50th anniversary gathering in 1949. It was one of the few photos that had anything written on the back to identify it. Her husband was Patrick Callahan, also from Ireland – J.P. McCormack had said in 1982 that Patrick was from Cloonfad. She and Patrick had nine children over the next 22 years, my father, Thomas Sr., being the fourth.

When I was a child my father showed me the tiny house in Lebanon Springs, NY that his family had rented from the Mount Lebanon Shaker Community for $5.00/month and told me stories of when he and his siblings had walked up the mountain on rent day to pay one of the Shakers who sat at a table out near the road. My grandfather had worked for the Rutland Railroad, a one track line that ran through Vermont from the Canadian border south to Chatham, NY, a modest village where three railroads intersected: the Rutland, the Boston and Albany and the New York Central. Most of the business on the Rutland consisted of milk and lumber supplies going to Chatham and thence to Albany, Boston and New York City. In 1918 the family moved to Chatham, first renting an apartment almost next to the tracks where the Rutland terminated, and later moving about a mile to a small house on the other side of the village, but still within a stone's throw of the tracks. The house in Lebanon Springs, my father said, had been bought by the Griffins, who were somehow related to us – though he seemed unsure exactly how – and their descendants still lived there.

I remembered the house in Chatham where the extended family had gathered on Christmas for some years. My parents and I lived locally, so we were there more often. I was the youngest of the five grandchildren and in the late-1940's the only "kid" at their gatherings. Bored with adult conversation, I explored the house, which didn't take long since there were only four rooms other than the kitchen, which was downstairs. In fact, most of my early memories of my grandparents, uncles and aunts are of the tops of their heads from the perspective of a metal grate in the floor of my grandparents' bedroom where I spied on the folks below. I later learned that the grate was there to distribute rising warm air because the house had no central heating. The house also had no indoor bathroom, so I was often anxious to get home. Patrick and Catherine seemed very old to me, which, indeed, they were. In the 1940s 70 wasn't "the new 50." I never really thought of them as being from a foreign country, though I was fascinated by my grandmother's soft lilting voice and my grandfather's accent that was so thick I could hardly understand him. I got to know my grandmother a little better a year or so before she died when she stayed with us for a couple of weeks after having fallen and broken her elbow. She slept in my room on my bed while I slept on the floor – a great adventure when you're 5. I also remember her complaining about her arthritis, though I had no idea at the time what that was. When she died of a heart attack soon after Christmas in 1952, my grandfather continued to live at their house with his youngest son, Timothy, who was always called Ted, until a few months before he died in a local nursing home five years later. Ted continued to live in the house for another dozen years until his premature death from cancer at age 50.

Catherine and Patrick left little behind save their children. When the house was cleaned out prior to being sold, my father removed whatever was of any value to be distributed among his surviving siblings. It didn't amount to much – some flatware, a few pieces of cheap jewelry, and some furniture. Two old steamer trunks came down from the attic, one with "K. T. McCormick" stenciled on one end. My father said that these were the trunks that had contained all the worldly possessions that his parents had brought from Ireland. I paid little attention to any of these things, for I had already grabbed in 1957 the only item that interested me, my grandfather's blackthorn walking stick, an iconic shillelagh which he had brought from Ireland and which I had coveted for as long as I could remember.

Looking back now, even the comparatively recent fifty years since my grandparents' possessions were scattered among their children, or, for the most part, consigned directly to the dump, seems like a far distant age. What must it have been like, well over a half-century earlier, for them to leave their homes and families to travel to America? Here were two farm kids, barely 20, uprooted from a traditional way of life that had not changed much for centuries, sailing to an uncertain future. Both had family already in the United States, so they would not be alone. Still, they and their siblings, both Callaghans and McCormacks, would have to make their way in a land unlike anything they had ever known.

Chapter 5
Those who left and those who stayed

Kate was excited to be returning home after three decades in America. She would be gone for nearly two months, and she was thrilled at the prospect of seeing the old cottage again, her two brothers and sister who had remained behind and her cousins and childhood friends. She looked forward to meeting the seven nieces and nephews whom she had never seen. Kate was nearly 52-years old, had nine children and a granddaughter. Daughter Eleanor was only seven, but 16-year old Mary could look after her for a few weeks. It was now or, probably, never. Pak couldn't get away, plus they could barely afford one fare, let alone two. Her sister-in-law Madge, who had been back home five years earlier, would accompany her. Kate got her passport, and off they went. What would it be like? How much had things changed? Martin and Maggie had been only 15 and 11 when she last saw them; now they were married with children of their own.

Arriving in Frenchpark on a cold December day, Kate was warmly greeted by family and friends. She was the first of the "Yanks" to come home, and spent hours talking and delivering messages and gifts from her American siblings. Mother and father had been dead for years, but everyone else was fine. She could only stay for one night at the cottage, as Mary Ann was about to give birth to her fifth child, but other relatives lived nearby. Madge went off to Cloonfad to visit with her Callaghan kin. Over the next few days Kate made the rounds, meeting friends and sending post cards of fair scenes in neighboring Ballaghaderreen to Pak and the children. She couldn't resist asking Mary "How do you like housekeeping?" When little Willie was baptized a couple weeks later, Kate stood as one of his sponsors.

Soon, too soon, came the time to depart. Kate wistfully recalled her American wake some 30 years before and her excitement and anxiety then at leaving home. This time, she knew, would be her final departure. She would never again see James or Martin, Mary Ann, Margaret or her husband Tom. Her nieces and nephews crowded around to say goodbye and thank you again for the chocolates she had

brought; she hoped they might remember her. Then she was off again to
Dublin and Queenstown, now called by its Irish name, Cobh, and the
ship to America. She and Madge, happy not to be in steerage on this
trip, spent Christmas at sea and joined in the shipboard New Year's
celebration ushering in 1929 the day before the Baltic docked in New
York.

As she sat on the train, looking out the window at the frozen
Hudson on her way home to Chatham, Kate was happy that she had
made the pilgrimage back to Roscommon, but was also convinced that
she had done the right thing thirty years earlier.

The United States that welcomed the McCormacks and millions
of other immigrants was a country engaged in a profound
transformation from a rural to an urban society. After the Civil
War, rapid industrialization caused massive urban growth while
improved transportation made it possible to feed and supply
rapidly expanding city populations. Especially on the east coast,
many of these cities became the new homes for a rising tide of
immigrants.

The first large surge of Irish had arrived as a result of The
Famine in mid-century. Streaming into New York and Boston as
well as smaller ports, these ragtag refugees took their places in
the bottom layer of white society. Often eyed with deep
suspicion by earlier immigrants, even the Protestant Irish who
now considered themselves "natives," the Famine exiles took
whatever jobs they could get. Being Catholic was also a
drawback in the United States where Protestants saw
Catholicism as antithetical to freedom and democracy. Whatever
the given rationale might have been, in truth many Americans
simply feared the Irish or looked down on them because they
were "different." It did not help that a large segment of the early
arrivals, being from the Gaelic west, could not read or write
English. The great majority of Irish immigrants had been farmers
at home, but the profession least attractive to them proved to be
farming. So, instead of moving on inland from the cities to

occupy the rich agricultural lands being opened in the west, most men stayed in the cities and took jobs in factories or on the railroads. Irish women increasingly filled the ranks of maids, servants and governesses in the households of the American middle class.

By the time that the McCormacks arrived in the United States, the Irish had become much more assimilated into American society. During the last three decades of the 19th Century the Irish were beginning to be regarded as more native than foreign. Rabid fear of Catholicism, at least in the northern states had dissipated, and the earlier characterizations of the Irish as drunken loafers had largely faded away. Irishmen worked on the railroads, in factories, and, as their numbers grew their political clout increased in eastern cities. Irish political "machines" were emerging, opening vast areas of public jobs on police forces, fire brigades and other municipal departments. Many Irish women who worked in upper-middle class homes learned the ways and manners of middle class America and passed these on to their children. Catholic parochial schools soon appeared in every city, and parents pushed their children to get good educations. The Irish percentage of newly arriving immigrants was falling rapidly as millions poured in from eastern and southern Europe. From a high of over 42% in 1850, Irish arrivals comprised just over 10% by 1900.[1] In the "melting pot" of America, the Irish were nearly assimilated. Still, each arriving immigrant from the island had to find their way, some with a good deal of help and some on their own, in what was to them a strange new world.

The McCormacks in America

All of the McCormack siblings who left Ireland in the late-19th century originally came to New Jersey. Five of the six remained and established their families there, almost all of them in West Orange. Today, West Orange, in fact all of the "Oranges" – West, East and South, as well as Orange itself, are part of the suburban

---

[1] Schrier, *Ireland*, 59, table 5.

sprawl that surrounds the cities of New York and Newark. Around 1900, however, these communities were more distinct. Comprising two ridges of the Watchung Mountains and the valley between, the town has some lovely parks that make it distinctive, though much of its individuality has disappeared over the decades. It was officially established in 1863 when some prominent local residents, dissatisfied with the public schools in Orange, petitioned the state legislature to form a separate township.[2] The new municipality and East Orange as well were carved out of the larger town of Orange, that had itself been separated from Newark a half century earlier.

At first West Orange was quite separate from larger surrounding communities, especially Newark, not having any horse or steam railway connections yet established.[3] The population grew steadily over the decades, reaching just over 6,000 by 1900 and more than 15,000 by 1920.[4] It increased further to some 40,000 by the end of the 20th century. As time went on and public transportation grew, West Orange became a popular bedroom community for the wealthy who wished to escape the growing city of Newark. In fact, much of the political maneuvering in the late-19th and early 20th centuries centered around efforts to keep Newark from reaching out and swallowing up the Oranges. Republicans who detested and feared the growing Democratic political machine, campaigned vigorously to remain separate from "Greater Newark."[5]

When reliable and reasonably priced trolley systems reached West Orange, they also brought with them increasing numbers of working class citizens. Many of these, like the first McCormacks, were employed by the wealthy Republicans up on the hill. Over the years industrial employment also came to

---

[2] J. Nole, *West Orange* (Charleston SC: Arcadia Books, 1998), 2.
[3] For history of West Orange NJ see J. Folsom, ed., *The Municipalities of Essex County 1666-1924* (New York: Lewis, 1925), II, 761-770.
[4] Ibid., 764, 770.
[5] J. Schwartz, "Suburban Progressivism," in J. Schwartz and D. Prosser, eds., *Cities of the Garden State: Essays in the Urban and Suburban History of New Jersey* (Dubuque: Kendall, 1977), 54.

town. There were hat manufacturers and, most significantly, Edison Industries. In 1886 Thomas Edison moved to West Orange and bought Glenmont, a stately mansion in Llewellyn Park. He built what was then the largest and best equipped research laboratory in the world a short distance away. The research facility had several permanent employees, but the largest source of employment at Edison Industries became the factory, which produced phonographs, records and batteries. These facilities provided work for many of the second generation of McCormacks as clerks and stock boys when they were just beginning their working lives.

The first of the family to arrive in America was John McCormack, the eldest child of Patrick McCormack and Catherine Keenan, born on the last day of March 1862. At some point after his arrival he changed the spelling of his name to McCormick, launching that variant among all his descendants. There is no family story about why he emigrated, but the reasons are most likely the same as for most others in his generation of Irish men. Conditions at home were difficult; by the time of his arrival, all eleven of his siblings had been born, and nine had survived. There was no tradition in Ireland that the eldest son would inherit the farm, and even if there had been, that event might well be decades in the future. Without land of his own John could not marry, and by the 1880s the days of land subdivision among children had long ended. So, John was faced with the same choices as millions of others – stay home and work as a laborer on his father's or some neighbor's farm, travel to England for seasonal labor if any could be found, or emigrate. He chose to leave, and picked New Jersey as his destination. It is not certain, but probable, that John chose New Jersey, and the city of West Orange, because of a childhood friend and neighbor, Peter Duignan, who had left Ireland before him in 1875. When John and his family first appear on the United States census, in 1900, they lived at 14 Llewellyn Avenue in West Orange. He had purchased a building lot there for $300.00 in 1891 and soon built a house which served the family for over a century.[6] Peter Duignan's family lived just two houses away.

It is important to note that Irish emigration patterns were frequently shaped by family and other personal connections. When family members crossed the Atlantic, they often settled close to their relatives who had preceded them. The same holds true for townland connections. Americans, even Irish-Americans, often find the concept of townlands baffling. They are the smallest official subdivision of land in Ireland, smaller than the civil parish, barony and county. Most date from pre-Norman times. The McCormacks were from the townland of Slieveroe in the civil parish of Castlerea in the barony of Frenchpark in County Roscommon. Probably the closest American equivalent in size would be a neighborhood. Slieveroe consisted of 220 acres, 47 of which were bog land, occupied by fifteen families totaling 64 people in the 1901 Irish census.[7]

Since John and Peter had certainly known each other in their small closely-knit townland back home, it is reasonable to conclude that it was just not a coincidence that when John came to America they lived on the same short street in West Orange. They also shared the same occupation after their arrival, gardeners. Llewellyn Avenue dead-ends at the border of Llewellyn Park, originally some 750 acres, America's first gated community and home to West Orange's elite, including Thomas Edison. Peter worked there as a gardener on the Chubb estate.[8]

Other familiar Slieveroe family names also appear in the official records for West Orange, further illustrating the phenomenon of chain migration. Bernard Farrell lived at 63 Llewellyn.[9] Michael Farrell, one of his Slieveroe ancestors, had

---

[6] Bill of Sale, John McCormack from Mary Sullivan, 14 August 1891. Collection of P. Davis.

[7] National Archives, Ireland, 1901 Census, Roscommon/Frenchpark/Slieveroe.

[8] D. Quinn, *The Irish in New Jersey* (New Brunswick: Rutgers University Press, 2004), 170.

[9] U.S. Department of the Interior, Town of Orange, Essex County, New Jersey, Enumeration District 184, Sheet 19, "Farrell, Bernard."

been a sub-tenant of the McCormacks in 1857.[10] Martin Brennan, another descendant of former McCormack sub-tenants, lived just up the street from the Duignans.[11] Patrick Dowd from the townland lived nearby on Park Terrace.[12] Peter Mahon ran a saloon on Main Street.[13] There were Morrisroes from the neighboring townland of Cartronbeg who were related to the Farrells and lived in Patrick McCormack's former house at 16 Llewellyn after his widow and children moved to nearby McKinley Avenue.[14] Several Sharkeys from the neighboring townland of Cloonfad lived nearby on Cross Street and High Street.[15] So John McCormack settled in America among friends.

In 1888, when he was still living near the corner of Joyce Street and Valley Road, John married Anne Morrisroe, from a neighboring townland, who, according to family lore, had come to West Orange with this wedding in mind. Anne's brother John, also a gardener, later lived with his family on Llewellyn Avenue between the McCormicks and the Duignans. Over the next fifteen years John and Anne had seven children, the second of whom died in infancy.

During his first decade in America John worked as a gardener, coachman and caretaker for Simeon Rollinson, a prominent West Orange lawyer who later served as mayor. In 1897 Rollinson wrote him a general letter of recommendation praising his good character and calling him "...absolutely sober, honest and industrious."[16] It is unknown whether John left Rollinson's employ at this time, but around 1905 he secured a

---

[10] Great Britain, Office of the General Valuation of Ireland, Valuation Lists for Roscommon County, Castlerea Rural District, 1850-1942, Slieveroe,1857, "Catherine McCormack/Martin Brennan/ Michael Farrell."

[11] Ibid.; U.S. Department of the Interior, City of Orange, Essex County, New Jersey, Enumeration District 161, Sheet 11, "Martin C. Brennan."

[12] Ibid., West Orange Town, Enumeration District 185, Sheet 20, "Patrick Dowd."

[13] Ibid., City of Orange, Essex County, New Jersey, Enumeration District 160, Sheet 16, "Peter Mahen [sic]."

[14] Ibid., West Orange Town, Essex County, New Jersey, Enumeration District 185, Sheet 21, "John Morrisrow [sic]."

[15] Ibid., City of Orange, Enumeration District 309, Sheet 14, "Patrick Sharkey."

[16] Letter, Simeon Rollinson to John McCormick, 5 June 1897. Collection of P. Davis.

better job with more security and higher pay on the West Orange police force. There is a striking photo of him around this time in his uniform sporting badge #8. He worked as a police officer for the next quarter century, retiring around 1930. During the Irish war of independence, John and his wife were ardent supporters of Sinn Fein and the rebels, contributing generously to the first loan drive in America in 1920 supporting the new Republic of Ireland.[17]

John and Anne also sent gifts home to support family in Ireland. Letters attest to their receipt and express gratitude for their kin's generosity. After retirement, John lived quietly at home and died of heart disease complicated by acute bronchitis at age 75 in October 1937. A letter the next month from his wife Anne's brother Patrick demonstrates the realistic Irish attitude toward death. "It is too bad about John's death," Pat wrote, "but that is the end of all of us."[18]

John's younger brother Patrick arrived next. The year is unknown, but it was 1888 at the latest, for he was a witness at John's wedding. He, too, worked as a gardener, probably in Llewellyn Park, as he and his family lived next door to John. Patrick had been born in 1866, just after a brother also named Patrick had died. His parents had re-used the name, probably because it was his father's name as well. In 1892 he married Delia Callaghan, my grandfather's older sister, whom he had surely known back home. Although they were from different townlands, they had attended the same church in Tibohine, just outside of Frenchpark. Whether they intended to marry when they emigrated is unknown.

The history of Patrick and his family is tragic. He and Delia had four children in rapid succession between 1893 and 1897 when Patrick was diagnosed with Bright's Disease, a term used in the 19th Century to describe acute nephritis which attacks the kidneys. In a few short months he was dead, leaving Delia in

<hr>

[17] Receipt, Irish Republic, 1920. Collection of P. Davis.
[18] Letter, Patrick Morrisroe to Anne McCormick, 26 November 1937. Collection of P. Davis.

August 1897, with four small children to care for and no family breadwinner. In the wake of this calamity Delia moved with her children to western Massachusetts, where many of her Callaghan relatives had settled. Accompanying her was Patrick's younger sister Catherine, known as Kate, who had arrived in America only a few months before Patrick's death. Kate would be the only one of the McCormack siblings to settle outside of New Jersey. We do not know why she went, but it was probably to help Delia care for the children. They traveled to Pittsfield, a small city on the Massachusetts-New York border and stayed with some of Delia's relatives. There, Kate became reacquainted with Delia's younger brother Patrick Callaghan, whom she had known at home since they both attended the same church. Patrick, or Pak, as Kate always called him, had a good job on the railroad. Less than two years later, in September 1899, they were married in New Lebanon, just over the border in New York. Delia and her children moved from Pittsfield and lived with them in a small rented cottage for at least a year.

Sometime between 1900 when the census shows them in Lebanon Springs and 1910 when the next survey found them back on Llewlleyn Avenue, Delia's family suffered a second tragedy, the death of her second son, Patrick Joseph, who had been born in 1894. Patrick, more usually called Joseph, had been born with some sort of serious disability. We do not know the exact nature of the problem, which was described by contemporaries as a bone disease. Delia remained a single mother to her surviving children for fifty years until her own death in 1947. Before then, in 1929, her eldest child, Thomas, known by his middle name Melvin, Delia's mother's maiden name, had also died, from a wasting mental illness. It is interesting to speculate how she managed to support herself and her children after Patrick's death. She may have had some financial help from Patrick's brothers, and her children went to work early to contribute as well, plus Delia took in laundry to help pay the bills.

The McCormack siblings came to America in the order of their birth. John was the eldest, Patrick, four years younger, and next was Thomas, born in 1870. James, born two years earlier, stayed in Ireland all his life. Thomas arrived at age 20 in 1890 and may have been the first of the brothers to eschew gardening as a new career. The fact that he did not live near his brothers on Llewellyn Avenue is one clue supporting this conclusion, plus on his 1900 marriage certificate he lists his occupation as "coachman."[19] Not much more is known about him before 1900 except that he was a witness at Patrick's wedding in 1892. There is also a splendid photo of him as a young man taken sometime in the mid-1890s.

In 1900 Thomas married Annie Hoare, an Irish immigrant from Longford, who worked as a maid in Newark, and they took up residence on Valley Road in West Orange. They had their only child, William J. McCormack, two years later. Presumably Thomas continued to work as a coachman for a few more years, but in 1909 he joined the West Orange police force, perhaps with the assistance of his brother John. Eventually they moved to Riggs Place in West Orange, and Thomas remained on the force for some twenty years before his retirement.

In 1931 Thomas and Annie went home for a visit, the second and last of the siblings to do so. His sister Kate had returned to Frenchpark for a few weeks at the end of 1928. Thomas and Annie traveled from Cobh to Longford, where Annie stayed a while with her family while Thomas went on home to visit his brothers and sister. Annie joined him there a few days later. A niece, Mai Robinson, who was 10 at the time, remembers Thomas and her father Martin McCormack talking one day out by the turf barn on the family homestead. She recalls being puzzled that they were both crying. When she asked her mother about this, she was told that they were sad because they knew that when Thomas returned to New Jersey they would never see each other

---

[19] New Jersey State Archives, Marriage Certificates and Indexes, Thomas McCormack/Anna Hoare, 25 April 1900, Essex County, M-167.

again. After he had left, Mai was told by her parents that he had wanted to take her with him to America.[20]

Seven years later, in June 1938, at age 68, Thomas became the third McCormack brother to die in America. Annie survived him for another decade.

A couple of years after Thomas arrived in New Jersey he was followed by his younger brother Michael, born in 1872. By outward appearances, he appears to have been the least successful of the American McCormacks, though not much detail is known about his life. He first appears in the historical record as an adult on the 1900 U.S. census as a coachman, one of many servants working for the Eugene Smith family in South Orange, NJ.[21] He had arrived in America seven years earlier. That same year he married Helen Higgins, an Irish immigrant living in Orange, and they moved to Ashland Avenue in West Orange. Michael soon got a job as a janitor at St. John's School in nearby Orange. Over the next seven years Michael and Helen had three children, a son and two daughters. In 1918 tragedy struck the family when Helen became one of the many victims of the influenza epidemic sweeping the country and died. None of their children married, two died young, and the last surviving daughter continued to live on her own at the family home on Ashland Avenue until her death around 1980. Michael himself died at age 69 in 1941.

I have already written a good deal about my grandmother, Catherine McCormack, the fifth sibling, and first female, to arrive in America. She had been the eighth child and the first daughter born to Patrick and Catherine. Not surprisingly, we know very little about her life before she came to America in 1897, though there exists a wonderful photograph showing her as a young teenager around 1890. The photo was taken outdoors, probably by an itinerant photographer. It is very likely that the

---

20 Interview with Mai McCormack Robinson, 24 January 2010.
21 US Department of the Interior, Twelfth Census, South Orange, Essex County NJ, Enumeration District 188, Sheet 18B, s.v. "McCormick, Michal."

location was actually the McCormack cottage, since the setting is clearly impromptu. In the center is her mother, Catherine Keenan McCormack, wrapped in a colorful shawl, looking very stern. On her right stands Katie, apparently right out of the kitchen, wearing her apron and a pair of well-worn, muddy, lace-up boots. On Catherine's left is little Martin, about 8 years old, wearing his best checked wool suit, but also with muddy shoes, and still carrying a stick with which he'd recently been playing. No one is smiling; having your picture taken in those days was serious business.

As I explained above, Kate came to America in April, 1897, the time of year when the vast majority of emigrants left Ireland. Presumably she arrived in New Jersey to join her brothers. Whether she planned to work right away or stay with one of them for a while is unknown. She listed her occupation on the manifest of the RMS *Campania* as "servant," but that was common with the vast majority of young female Irish immigrants. Soon, however, her brother Patrick died and Kate accompanied his widow, Delia, to Pittsfield, Massachusetts where she lived for a while with the Albon family. The tone of a letter addressed to her there in 1898 from an Albon daughter visiting California makes it unlikely that she was working as a family servant.[22]

The next certainty about her life is that she married Delia's younger brother, Patrick Callahan – at some point he had dropped the "g" from Callaghan – in September 1899 and moved to the tiny village of Lebanon Springs, just over the New York-Massachusetts border. The village existed largely because it had natural springs whose water was reputedly therapeutic. A small resort hotel was built next to them, and the Rutland railroad brought seasonal visitors to take the waters. Kate and Patrick, however, had nothing to do with this. Pak, as she called him, worked on a railroad section crew which had the responsibility for maintaining six miles of track. Each day he and his co-workers would walk that distance, checking for loose ties,

---

[22] Letter, Mollie Albon to Katie McCormack, 17 December 1898. Collection of author.

misaligned rails, and other problems. Delia and her four small children lived with them in Lebanon Springs for at least a year, so Kate had her hands full. Within a year of her marriage her first child, a girl they named Madeline, arrived, followed over the next 21 years by eight more, six boys and two girls, all healthy. Another studio photograph from around 1900 shows the scrawny, awkward, teenaged Katie now grown into a confident young woman in America.

In 1918, probably due to the need for more space, Kate and Pak moved about eighteen miles down the Rutland line to its terminus in Chatham, NY. There they rented an apartment on Park Row, some fifty feet from the Rutland station, for a few years before moving to Locust Street on the other side of the village. Their new house, probably some fifty-years old when they moved in, was on a steep street. When one walked in the front door at street level you were actually on the second floor, consisting of two tiny bedrooms, a small living room and a walk-in closet. Downstairs was the kitchen and one further bedroom. There was no indoor bathroom until a fire in 1950 necessitated some renovations. Their last child, Eleanor, was born in this house, and there Kate and Pak lived until their deaths.

By now, Pak was the foreman of the section crew, responsible for the entire roadbed between Chatham and Lebanon Springs. With the promotion came a bit more money and less heavy lifting. The older children began to move away as they found employment. Some of the boys got jobs on the railroad, and the oldest girl, Madeline, went off to Newark, NJ to work for Prudential Insurance. Kate kept in touch with her siblings in West Orange, which, though some 150 miles away, was easily reachable by train, and Pak's job came with a railroad pass that allowed them to travel for free. There are a number of period photos of Kate and Pak in West Orange, usually taken in the back yard of John's home at 14 Llewellyn Avenue. She always looked a bit shy, while Pak stood boldly with his legs spread, looking directly at the camera. Kate seemed to have been particularly close to her niece Anne McCormick, John's daughter. There are also photographs of John's widow and children visiting Kate and Pak in Chatham, showing that family travels went both ways.

In 1928, Kate decided to return home to Frenchpark for a visit. Although her youngest child was only 7, her middle daughter, Mary, was 16 and fully capable of looking after Eleanor and Ted, who was 9, plus cooking and cleaning for her father. Kate got a passport, which shows a photo of a middle-aged woman who has lived a life of hard work, and made arrangements to travel with one of Pak's younger sisters, Madge Sharkey, from West Orange. Madge had returned once before, in 1923, so was not only good company, but was also familiar with the return journey. They sailed at the beginning of November, probably because the fares were least expensive in the winter.

On their arrival on November 9th, Kate retraced the route she had traveled some 30 years before, but in reverse. Much had changed since she had last been home. Her older brothers, James and William, were in their 60s or nearly so. William was retired from the Royal Irish Constabulary and now owned a hotel up in Donegal, but James still farmed, though not his own land. In fact, when his youngest brother Martin had finally inherited the farm, James chose to leave home and live instead with his youngest sister's family a mile or so away. Martin and Margaret, her younger siblings, were now married and each had children whom Kate would meet for the first time. Her parents were long dead, but Kate had not really expected to ever see them again. The homestead, a two room thatched cottage, had hardly changed at all. Compared to it, Kate's little house in Chatham looked grand.

Kate had arrived at a bad time for entertaining. The weather was cold, wet and miserable and Mary Ann was about to give birth to her last child, William Joseph, in a few days and was not feeling well. So Kate only stayed one night with them, as her niece Mai McCormack Robinson recalled over 80 years later.[23] Still her visit was welcomed, especially by the children. Another

---

[23] Interview with Mai Robinson, 24 January 2010.

niece, Sr. Joseph, nee Bridget McLoughlin, still remembers that her Aunt Kate brought them chocolates from America.

Instead, she and Madge went to lodge with the Callaghans in Cloonfad, just down the road. Kate soon traveled to the market fair in the sizable town of Ballagadereen a few miles away and purchased, as tourists do, some picture post cards to send home. She sent Teddy a card of Market Street and wrote "What do you think of this, Teddy dear? Lots of love from Mother." On Mary's she asked "How do you like housekeeping? Oceans of love, Mother." To her husband Pak she sent a card showing the market fair itself, writing "I went to this fair, had a good time. Lots to tell you about it when I get home. Love from Kate."[24]

Kate and Madge left just before Christmas to return home. They had planned to leave earlier, but had cancelled their original reservations to stay on an extra week. They may have stopped over at the Globe Hotel in Dublin, for Kate kept one of their business cards in a box of her valuables. They boarded the SS Baltic on 23 December and celebrated both Christmas 1928 and New Year's 1929 on board before their arrival in New York on January 2nd. Madge took a train home to West Orange, and Kate sent Pak a telegram announcing her return and made her way to Grand Central Station to catch a New York Central train to Chatham

Pak retired in 1938 and he and Kate settled into quiet lives on Locust Street. The house had no central heating, but there were two kerosene heaters, one upstairs in the living room and the other in the kitchen. As I mentioned above, there was no indoor toilet, but they had never had one in their lives so missed it much less than we would. Pak spent much of his time in the kitchen, where it was the warmest, drinking tea out of the saucer, rather than the cup, and smoking his ubiquitous corncob pipe. He was also fond of reciting tales in a dramatic voice of legendary Irish heroes, both in prose and poetry, whether you wanted to hear them or not. During World War II they kept wary eyes on the

---

[24] Three postcards mailed 1 December 1928 from Ballaghaderreen. Collection of author.

news, as one son, Andy, was in the Pacific and another, Ted, in the European theatre. If a messenger arrived with a telegram bordered in black, it would contain the worst possible message. They were overjoyed when both sons returned safely. In 1945 Andy sent his mother a letter containing a small Japanese silk fan from Tokyo, apologizing for such a small gift, but adding "I wanted to get you something nicer, but things are kind of a mess here."[25]

Kate's health slowly deteriorated after the war. She had increasing heart problems, and her arthritis, which had plagued her for years, made her hands almost unusable. On December 28th, 1952 she succumbed to a heart attack at the age of 76. Pak was inconsolable. He lived in the house on Locust Street for another five years with his youngest son Ted, but was finally moved to a local nursing home and died a few weeks later at age 84 of what his death certificate described as "general arteriosclerosis," but which my father simply called "old age."

The last of the McCormack siblings to relocate in America was the second daughter, Bridget, better known as Beatrice, who had been born in 1883. In 1901 she was still living at home with her mother, younger sister and two elder brothers, but by 1903 she had left, gotten married to an Englishman, Ernest Daniels, and had settled in Newark, NJ. It is unknown how or where she and Ernest met. In 1910 they were servants in the large Robert Crabb household in Newark, she as a maid and he as a coachman.[26] In 1911 their first son, Ernest, Jr. was born, followed in 1914 by William. At some point during this period the family moved out of the Crabb household, though Ernest may have continued to work there, as the family continued to live in Newark, and he is

---

[25] Letter, Andrew Callahan to Kate Callahan, 23 October 1945. Collection of author.
[26] US Department of the Interior, Newark City, Essex County, NJ, Enumeration District 237, Sheet 1-A, s.v. "Daniels, Beatrice."

listed as a private chauffeur in both the 1920 and 1930 census. Their only daughter, Mary, was born in 1921.

Bea returned to active child raising during World War II when Mary's husband, Harry Franklin, was killed in action in Europe, leaving her with an infant daughter. In a 1949 letter home to her brother Martin, Bea complains that she has no time to do what she would like to do because "…this youngster keeps me busy."[27] Plus, after the child goes to bed, Bea was too tired to do much. Her husband Ernest was also having health problems at this time, suffering acute pain from frequent gall bladder attacks. Clearly frustrated, she wrote: "So you see, my troubles never end, just troubles and worries, no matter what country you're in."[28]

During this period she also sent hard-to-find goods to Martin's family and began to make plans to have Martin's youngest son, Willie, emigrate to the United States. He would have been the first McCormack in a half century to make the transition from Ireland to America. These plans, unfortunately, came to naught when Willie died from a brain aneurism when he was just 22.

By 1953 Bea was the last of the emigrants still living. She survived for another seventeen years, dying at age 87 in 1970. In her later years she associated most closely with her younger sister Margaret's children, Paddy and Maureen, who had come to America in the late-1940s. They knew her as Auntie Bea, but knew little of her siblings or their families.

[27] Letter Bea Daniels to Martin McCormack, 25 April 1949. Collection of C. Carr.
[28] Ibid.

Patrick McCormack, Anne and John McCormick at John and Anne's Wedding 1888

Patrick McCormack c. 1892

Thomas McCormack c. 1895

Thomas and Annie McCormack Wedding 1900

Michael and Helen McCormack Wedding 1900

John McCormick West Orange Police 1910

Catherine McCormack Callahan 1930

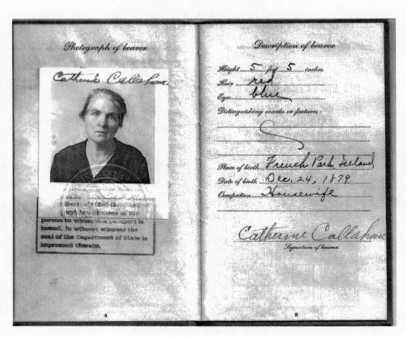

Catherine Callahan Passport 1928

Catherine and Tom Callahan, Jr. 1945

Bridget McCormack Daniels 1905

THE McCORMACKS IN IRELAND

The primary asset for any Irish farm family was land, the source of their livelihood and security. We have looked earlier at some of the general issues and controversies involving landholding in the 19th century. While only an extremely small percentage of farmers owned their farms even at the end of the century, most families had fairly secure tenure with annual or even multi-year leases from the wealthy landlords. Tenure could be inherited, even if one did not actually own the land.

By the late-19th century, the British government was becoming increasingly frustrated with seemingly intractable Irish problems. The Land League caused intermittent uproars, and rent strikes and even rural violence were increasing. Under these circumstances the government proposed a series of land acts to improve conditions for Irish farmers and calm the populace. One of the most important features of these acts was a plan to persuade or even compel landlords to break up their large estates and sell the land to their tenants.

In addition, the government created the Congested Districts Board in the Land Act of 1891. This body was to deal with the serious problems, especially in the unfertile west, of there being too many small farms to be efficient and profitable and too many poor people depending on meager resources. The Board's activities were many and varied, including holding classes on improved agricultural techniques, but the main activity that was crucial to the McCormacks and their neighbors was the Board's purchase of large estates and their redistribution among the local farmers. At first, the policy was to offer incentives to the landlords to entice them to make the transition voluntarily. By the early-20th century, the Wyndham Act of 1903 gave the Congested Districts Board the authority to compel the sales.

An examination of the tax records for the McCormack farm demonstrates this policy. When they married in 1861, Patrick McCormack and his wife Catherine Keenan, as well as all their neighbors in Slieveroe, rented their farms from John French, Baron de Freyne. Originally, they retained the same two sub-tenants, Martin Brennan and Michael Farrell, who had been there when the Griffith's Valuation was conducted in 1857. By 1866, however, the sub-tenants were gone, and Patrick farmed the whole seven acre property himself. Nothing changed in regard to the farm's rental status, size or rent for nearly forty years.

In 1900 Patrick died, and the tax valuation list reflects this by the crossing out of his name and writing in Catherine's in 1901.[29] Another change was that an additional acre of land was acquired, bringing the total now to eight. Then, substantial changes began. In 1910 Catherine was one of the first in her townland to benefit from the Wyndham Act by having her landlord changed from Baron de Freyne to the Congested Districts Board, signaling that the family's transition from renters to owners had begun. The next year saw a 50% increase in the farm's size, from eight to twelve acres, echoing the Board's efforts to increase farm size to promote prosperity. Somewhere around the time of Catherine's death in 1915, the transition was completed, and the new mortgage payments were actually less than the original rent payments from the middle of the previous century.[30] Against this background, let us take a look at the lives of those family members who remained in Ireland

---

THE "HOMEPLACE"

First, we need to look at the McCormack ancestral farm, what the Irish then, and now, refer to as the "homeplace." As we have seen, land was crucially important to the Irish, as much of the country's economy depends on agriculture. Even today, Irish who have what we would call regular jobs, in the trades or even professional, often keep a few cattle or sheep on the side. Farms are rarely sold, so long as there is someone to inherit the land. So

---

[29] Great Britain, Office of the General Valuation of Ireland, Castlerea Rural District, 1850-1942. LDS, FHL British Films, v. 17 Electoral Division Frenchpark, 867977.
[30] Ibid.

today the McCormack homeplace is still in family hands, having been passed down from Patrick and Catherine to their youngest son Martin, from him to his only surviving son John P., and from John to his sister Beatie's son James Dowd.

The twelve acres inherited by Martin in 1915 has since grown to twenty-one with the purchase of nine acres by his son John P. The sort of farming done has changed a bit over the years. In the 19th and early-20th Centuries, the McCormacks engaged in mixed farming, mainly raising cattle and sheep, but also keeping pigs, chickens and other livestock. Now the farm is used to raise what are called "dry" cattle, that is, cattle raised for a year or so to sell at market rather than cows raised for milking.

The homeplace is located on a low rise reached by a dead-end country lane just off the road which passes the abandoned Cloonmagunnaun national school, attended by most of the first and second generation McCormack children, a short five minute walk away from home. There were four houses on the short lane, only the first of which is still inhabited. The next two are complete ruins. At the McCormack farm, the house where J. P. lived still stands, but has been vacant since his death in 2001.

Set back about 100 yards from the lane, the house is flanked by a variety of structures of different ages. Immediately to the left and slightly to the rear is the site of the old whitewashed cottage with a thatched roof where J. P. and his siblings, their father Martin and his brothers and sisters were raised. As mentioned above, the house was demolished in the early 1950s when the new house was constructed. Its remains are still evident, and it seems nearly unbelievable now that twelve people once lived there. Abutting the remains is an equally old stone outbuilding now covered with a low corrugated steel roof. Behind these structures one can see small fields, separated by stone walls and hedgerows, where cattle graze.

About fifty feet farther left, on the same plane as the old house, a smaller and even older structure nestles among small saplings and tangled weeds. It too is made of loose stone and capped by a rusting corrugated roof. According to family lore, this small, low hut was once an earlier family home, perhaps dating back to the early 19th century. Without some sort of archeological investigation, however, we can never be certain about this structure's original purpose.

A walk around the homeplace today suggests a stark contrast between the lives of the six McCormack children who left for America and those of their parents, brothers and sister who stayed at home. While the emigrants encountered the hustle and bustle of growing American towns and cities, life went on as usual at home, though with fewer mouths to feed and fewer hands to help, for those who stayed.

Four of Patrick's and Catherine's children remained in Ireland while their siblings departed for America. Three, two sons and a daughter, remained on the farm with their parents while the fourth went off to begin a career in the Royal Irish Constabulary, the native Irish police employed by the British government. They kept in touch with their brothers and sisters in the United States, as evidenced by the few surviving photographs they sent to New Jersey. These images, combined with the memories of elderly descendants, depict lives very different from those who had left. Bridget's departure at the beginning of the last century came just before the time of escalating tensions in Ireland between the British government and the growing nationalist movement, leading inexorably to the Anglo-Irish War and the subsequent civil war in the early 1920s. Yet, for most of the McCormacks, life simply went on as before, in the traditional Irish manner, rooted in Slieveroe and neighboring townlands. For the young constable, however, a very challenging career lay ahead.

--

The eldest of those who stayed, James, has left a faint historical footprint. He was the third son, born in 1868. In the first surviving Irish census in 1901, James is found living at home with his mother and three younger siblings. His mother

Catherine, recently widowed at Patrick's death in 1900, is listed as the head of the family. The column headed "Education" reveals that James is illiterate, while his younger brother and two sisters can "read and write." Catherine herself can apparently read, perhaps both Irish and English. She cannot write, however, as she places an X, "her mark" witnessed by constable Gilligan, where the head of the family signed to attest to the accuracy of the census survey.[31] It is reasonable to conclude that James, as the eldest son by some sixteen years, was responsible for the day-to-day management of the farm at this time. He was single, as he could not marry without land of his own, and his mother was still the head of the family.

Ten years later, the next census shows that not much changed in the intervening decade. Catherine still heads the family, and James at 45, and his brother Martin at 29, are living at home and running the farm. Bridget, known also as Delia and, by posterity as Beatrice, had left Ireland, married and settled in New Jersey with her own family on the way. Catherine's youngest child, Margaret, is still on the farm, apparently taking in sewing, as she's listed as a "dressmaker." This census form is the last we see of James in any official venue until his death.

In 1915, the McCormacks mourned the loss of their mother when Catherine Keenan McCormack died two weeks after suffering a stroke at home. Apparently to James' dismay, the farm went to Martin, the youngest son. Martin soon married and James, though he had a traditional right to remain on the farm, chose instead to leave home and move in with his sister Margaret, who had recently married Tom McLoughlin, in Callow, a short distance away. Apparently, this incident caused a rift between the McCormacks and McLoughlins which lasted some 20 years. Mai Robinson, Martin's only surviving child, does not recall the estrangement and said that her Uncle James was always very friendly with her when she visited the McLoughlins. On the other hand, she can never recall James setting foot again

---

[31] National Archives of Ireland, 1901, Roscommon/Frenchpark/Slieveroe, House 6.

on the family farm. While in Callow, James helped with the farm work and also took other temporary jobs with local farmers to earn some extra money. Later in life he was quite crippled by rheumatism making it difficult for him to do manual labor. He spent much of his time in these years helping to raise the McLoughlin children. Sr. Joseph still recalls him rocking the cradle for her younger siblings. He was nursed through his final illness by his nephew Patrick. When he died in 1946, instead of being buried in the old Tibohine graveyard with his parents, brother William and two other brothers who died in infancy, James was interred instead in the McLoughlin plot at the old Killaraght cemetery with his sister and her husband.

We'll never know why Catherine chose to pass the farm on to Martin instead of to his older brother. Perhaps she decided that James, at 47 was too old to marry and start a family. Maybe the decision involved the fact that James was illiterate. Perhaps she perceived that Martin was simply more capable of taking over and still young enough to marry and raise the next generation of McCormacks. Whatever the reason, the decision clearly rankled James for years to come. There is only one certain photo of him, a blurry snapshot of an old farmer who seemingly does not want his picture taken. There is one other possible photo, an earlier studio portrait of his mother in old age with one of her grown sons, either James or Martin. The poor quality of the photograph makes positive identification impossible.

--

James' younger brother William, six years his junior, also chose to remain in Ireland, but not as a farmer. Instead, at age 23 he enlisted in the Royal Irish Constabulary in 1898. Although he did not know it at the time, his career choice would place him right at the center of the impending struggle for Irish independence. RIC constables were seen by Irish nationalists as the agents of their English oppressors. Even worse, they were Irish and should, many thought, be on the other side of the fight.

In 1898, however, these dark clouds were not yet on the horizon. To be a constable was a definite step up for farmers' sons in rural Ireland. The position gave a young man status, a steady income and the prospect of a pension. It gave him authority, a uniform, a gun and all the other paraphernalia of police work. The job's financial security and social status also attracted young women who usually came from the same rural background and made constables attractive marriage prospects. At the end of the 19th century a government panel in the west of the island reported that some public houses were selling a concoction called White Rose to women keeping company with constables. An official recalled being told that "The girls do be puttin' it on their handkerchers ... if they're goin' walking out with the police... [I]t takes the smell of the turf out of their hair and clothes and gives them a great charrum."[32] Out in the countryside, where most of the constables worked, especially in the west, the Royal Irish Constabulary was one of the very few alternatives a man could have to low paying and usually dead end farm labor or emigration. In fact, William was the only non-emigrating McCormack brother to be something other than a farmer.

Joining the RIC was not easy. District authorities kept an eye out for intelligent able-bodied sons of respectable local farmers, but it could be years before one made it from the waiting list to actual service. Candidates had to be personally known to and judged to have high moral character by a local official or clergyman, whose name was entered next to the recruit's on the enlistment register. The minimum age was 19 unless you were the son of a serving constable, in which case it was lowered to 18. The maximum age by the time of William's enlistment was 27 and most constables entered service in their early 20s.[33] There were also strict physical standards, including sound health and a minimum height of 5' 9", except, again, for sons of RIC men where it was 5' 8". It was not unusual for a recruit to be tentatively accepted, only to be subsequently rejected by the examining physician until he got into shape. In fact, this

---

[32] B. Griffin, *The Irish Police 1836-1914: A Social History* (Chicago: Loyola University Press, 1991), 174-75
[33] E. Malcolm, *The Irish Policeman 1822-1920: A Life* (Dublin: Four Courts Press, 2006), 56.

happened to William who enlisted on 2 August 1898, only to be temporarily rejected upon his physical examination. He was re-appointed at the beginning of December, though with loss of pay for the intervening months. At 5' 9 ¼" he stood just over the minimum height.[34]

Once accepted for service, recruits were sent off to Dublin for a rigorous six months of intense military style training at the constabulary headquarters in Phoenix Park. It was commonly said that you could always tell an ex-RIC man, even in old age, by his erect posture and the precise way he walked. Finally trained and outfitted, constables were assigned to barracks scattered about the country where they lived while patrolling the countryside on bicycles and enforcing the law. There was a strict rule in the interest of impartiality that constables could not serve in their home counties, so William, from Roscommon, began his service in County Meath on the first of June 1899. From there he was transferred to Leitrim early in the new century.[35]

It was in Leitrim that William met his bride-to-be, Eliza Creamer. Eliza was six years older than William, had never been married, and was listed in the 1911 census as a farmer in Aghyowla townland. She was the head of household and lived with her younger widowed sister, a niece and a young farm servant. We do not know for certain how they met, but it could well have been in the course of William's official duties. Besides enforcing the law, RIC constables served also as government census takers. The 1911 form for Eliza Creamer and her household was signed by "William McCormack, Enumerator."[36] Five years later, on St. Valentine's Day 1916, William and Eliza wed. RIC regulations regarding marriage were very strict. They only accepted bachelors, or widowers who had no children, and constables could not subsequently wed without permission from

[34] Great Britain, Public Record Office, *Irish Constabulary, General Registers of Services, Returns of Personnel and Intelligence Notices, 1816-1922*, LDS Film 0852090, Service # 58,333, "William McCormack."

[35] Ibid.

[36] National Archives of Ireland, 1911 Census, Leitrim/Garadice/Aghyowla, House 3.

his county inspector. The prospective wife's family background was also examined to ensure that she was "respectable."[37] Plus, there was a minimum service requirement, usually seven years, before permission to marry could be sought. Their wedding mandated William's immediate transfer out of Leitrim to Tyrone, for not only could a constable not serve in his own home county, but also that of his wife.

William served in County Tyrone for the rest of his career. He and Eliza either lived in the barracks or secured lodgings within a quarter mile, as regulations required. Whichever the alternative, their lives were subject to close scrutiny by RIC officers who inspected their living quarters for neatness.[38] Wives were forbidden from engaging in many occupations, and they could not take in lodgers even if they lived outside the barracks. Any complaints about a wife's behavior could have serious consequences for a constable, including possible dismissal. Their marriage produced no children, probably because Eliza was already 48 at the time of their wedding.

William's last years in the RIC encompassed the most difficult and dangerous period in Irish police history. A few weeks after William's wedding, the ill-fated Easter Rising exploded in Dublin, proclaiming the birth of the Republic of Ireland. The rebellion had been simmering for decades during which nationalist sentiments had increased dramatically. Yet, right up until the first shots were fired at the central post office, most of the Irish population had supported a peaceful constitutional path to separation from Great Britain. Home Rule, rather than complete independence, was favored by the majority of Irish citizens, who saw the example of Canada, firmly in control of its own internal affairs, but still professing loyalty to the king, as the best path. Under Prime Minister Gladstone in the previous century, a number of home rule bills had been voted on in Parliament, and each time the goal seemed closer. But, there

---

[37] Griffin, *Irish Police*, 168.
[38] Ibid, 173.

were powerful foes, both in England and northern Ireland to any change in the island's status.

In England, members of the Conservative party decried the prospect of home rule as signaling the first step toward the dissolution of the British Empire and vowed never to let it happen. In northern Ireland where Protestant plantations since the 17th century had supplanted Catholic majorities, political leaders feared being set adrift in a Catholic sea if the island regained even the partial political autonomy lost with the Union in 1800. Yet, when the Liberals regained the majority in Parliament in the early-20th century it looked as though Home Rule was finally at hand. Legislation passed the Commons stripping the House of Lords, the main bastion of English Conservatism, of the power to veto laws passed by the House of Commons for more than two years. And, finally, the Third Home Rule Bill was passed by the Commons for the third time in 1914 and received the king's assent on 15 September. The bill mandated the establishment of an all-Ireland parliament in Dublin with control of all government powers except defense and foreign policy. Irish jubilation was muted, however, for World War I had begun a month earlier, postponing the actual implementation of home rule for the duration.

In the early years of the war it became apparent that the Protestants in the northern counties were prepared to do whatever they thought necessary to prevent home rule. The Orange Order raised and illegally armed militias to be mobilized in the event of the bill's implementation and Conservative politicians in England recklessly vowed to support them at any cost to preserve the empire. In the south, as the prospect of a peaceful transition to self-government faded, militant nationalists became bolder in their assertion of the need for armed rebellion, either because they thought it necessary, or because it would be more fitting for Ireland to seize its independence rather than be given a luke-warm version of it by the English imperialists. When British troops became bogged down in the trenches of France early in the war, militants in the

IRB and IRA decided that it was time to act and proclaimed Irish independence in Dublin on Easter Monday, 1916.

The results of this futile uprising are well known. Most Irish were shocked and appalled at what seemed to be a foolish if not treacherous act when many Irish troops were fighting in France. It did not help that the rebels made favorable references to Germany in their proclamation. Within a week order had been restored, though Dublin had suffered considerable damage. Then the British officer in charge in Ireland made a major blunder by trying and executing fifteen of the rebel leaders over the course of a week. The patriotic speeches that the condemned made at their trials inflamed Irish resentment against the British and turned their pitiful military failure into a major moral victory. When World War I ended and general elections were held again, Redmond's Irish Party, which had championed the cause of home rule, was swept from Parliament in 1918 by the more radical and pro-independence party, Sinn Fein. The newly-elected MPs refused to take their seats at Westminster and set up instead an independent Irish parliament, the Dail Eireann, in Dublin in January 1919. The Dail then issued a Declaration of Independence, precipitating the Anglo-Irish War which lasted for two years.

This war put the members of the Royal Irish Constabulary in an extremely difficult position. They were the policing arm of the British government in Ireland, but they were also Irish. Michael Collins, who spearheaded the IRA's campaign against British occupation, concentrated the group's efforts against RIC men and their barracks. During the war, nearly two-thirds of the island's 1400 barracks where the constables and their families lived were either completely destroyed or made uninhabitable.[39] Letters were sent by the IRA to serving constables threatening them with ostracism or death if they did not resign. Many did leave the force, and many others were killed or wounded. Some constables covertly aided the rebels at considerable danger to

---

[39] Malcolm, *Irish Policeman*, 200.

themselves. Nearly 600 policemen died violently over the next three years and a further 700 were wounded.[40]

At the height of the Anglo-Irish War, William McCormack left the force after twenty-three years. His service record notes that he was pensioned from the RIC in June 1921, at age 47.[41] We do not know his reasons for leaving, though it is not difficult to imagine the pressures he and his fellow officers faced. He did not return to his home county or any of the counties where he had served. Instead, he and his wife Eliza moved to the sea-side town of Bundoran in Donegal where he bought and operated a hotel, Three Halls Place. Eliza died in the 1930s. William's own death came after an illness around 1940. During his last illness, he returned home to the farm and is buried near his parents in the Old Tibohine graveyard.

William's youngest brother, Martin, born in 1882, inherited the family farm in 1915 and carried on the McCormack name in the family in Ireland. He was the most photographed of the McCormack brothers in Ireland, probably because he lived the longest and had children. The photographs span nearly his entire life, beginning with his appearance around age eight with his mother and sister Katie and ending in the early 1950s shortly before his death. His images give the impression of a very serious man. His children remembered him as a kind and gentle father.

Martin inherited the farm and started his family during a very tumultuous time in Ireland. The Easter Rising had soon led to the rising popularity of Sinn Fein and the Anglo-Irish War of 1919-1921, the first serious challenge to British rule since the 18th century, and the first to not depend on foreign intervention for success. The war was essentially an insurgency with small bands of fighters sabotaging and burning English facilities and assassinating soldiers and police. As a result the English deployed more troops around the countryside, including the

---

[40] Ibid, 199.
[41] *Irish Constabulary, General Registers*, #58,333, "William McCormack."

hated "black and tans," hardened veterans of World War I sent to bolster the native RIC. There was fighting in Roscommon as elsewhere in the country, disrupting the economy and society.

We do not know what Martin's politics were or how the war affected his family, but having a brother in the RIC certainly would not have been an asset with the nationalists. Tensions eased a little when a truce was called in mid-1921 and negotiations began on a treaty to end the war. The outcome of these negotiations proved disastrous. It became apparent to the Irish delegation led by Michael Collins that the best that could be achieved without renewing the war – which he was convinced the Irish could not win militarily – was acquiescing to a divided Ireland and dominion status -- the Irish Free State. The acceptance of this status by the negotiators drove a wedge between those nationalists who demanded complete separation from Great Britain as the Irish Republic and those pragmatists like Collins who argued that they had obtained the "freedom to achieve freedom" by peaceful means.[42] A contentious election in 1922 won by Treaty supporters led to a brief but bloody civil war pitting the diehard IRA fighters against the Free State government. Collins, who led the government, was killed in an IRA ambush in August 1922, but the Free State soon crushed the opposition, forcing the IRA underground to bide its time.

The next decade in the Free State was a grim one. Much of Ireland's infrastructure had been damaged or destroyed in the wars, poverty was growing, and widespread emigration resumed. The government kept the structure and even many of the same officials from colonial days and strove to maintain fiscal responsibility above all. Conservative legislation pressed by the Catholic Church introduced new restrictions in Irish society, including censorship and the outlawing of divorce. Most Irish people had reasonably expected conditions to improve after the British had left, but were bitterly disappointed. In 1926 Eamon deValera, who had spearheaded opposition to the Treaty in 1921,

---

[42] T. W. Moody and F. X. Martin, *The Course of Irish History*, 4th ed. (Lanham, MD: Roberts Rinehart, 2001), 21.

quit Sinn Fein and began a new political party, Fianna Fail, which would come to dominate Ireland over the next several years.

When Fianna Fail won the election in 1932 and took over control of the Free State, de Valera began a decade of confrontational policies toward Britain which severely affected Irish farmers like Martin McCormack. Ireland was still profoundly rural, with over 61% of the population living on farms as late as 1926.[43] While the new leader's conservative Catholic social agenda was popular among the farmers, his economic policies wreaked havoc. Basically, de Valera was determined to sever as many of Ireland's ties to Britain as possible. So, in 1932 he unilaterally suspended the oath to the king which the Treaty implemented and stopped sending the semi-annual installments of the land annuity payments from Irish farmers to Britain. These payments were to reimburse the English for money advanced to renters since 1870 to buy their farms from landlords. Britain soon responded by placing tariffs on Irish agricultural goods imported into Britain. De Valera retaliated by instituting tariffs on British manufactured goods coming into Ireland.

The resulting economic war was ruinous for the Irish economy. It made Irish exports more expensive and hence less popular in Britain at the same time that it increased the prices of the British goods they needed to buy. So, because 96% of Irish exports went to Britain while only a small percentage of British imports came from Ireland, the impact on Ireland was dire, while on England, insignificant. Irish farm exports dropped from £35.8 million in 1929 to £13.5 million in 1935, with cattle exports especially hard hit.[44] The government hoped that the decrease in British imports would help stimulate the domestic economy to make up the difference, but positive results fell far short. Plus, Irish personal incomes lagged. In 1931 they had averaged 61% of their British counterparts, but had fallen to 49% by 1939.[45] Eventually, de Valera realized the folly of his policy and

---

[43] Ranelagh, *Short History*, 213.
[44] Ibid., 225.
[45] Ibid., 226.

accepted a generous compromise offer from Britain which allowed for a freer flow of Irish agricultural exports.

Then, as today, the most important farm product in Ireland was beef, especially in Connacht. Irish beef is especially prized because it is largely grass fed. The relatively mild Irish climate promotes nearly year-round grazing of cattle. The government under deValera attempted to increase Irish self-sufficiency in food production by reducing the emphasis on cattle, but the results were disappointing, as agricultural output actually decreased. During Martin's tenure, the farm was sufficient to support his large family, but was not what one would term prosperous. Only with the acquisition of additional acreage for grazing in the next generation did the farm's income measurably increase.

Like most Irish family farms, Martin's only rarely employed outside labor. His sons were his primary workforce, though the whole family had to pitch in to do what needed to be done. Even today, this is still the labor pattern prevalent in Irish agriculture. Family farms predominate and farming life goes on much as it did in previous generations, save with more mechanical help.

The youngest of the surviving McCormack siblings was Margaret, born in 1886. She was the only female to remain at home and marry. According to census data, in 1901 she had still been at school and in 1911 she was recorded as a dressmaker, which probably meant that she took in sewing at home. When she was 28 she married a local farmer, Tom McLoughlin, a widower whose first wife and a child had died in childbirth. They lived in Callow, a townland very close to her family home. In the summer of 1915 Margaret rejoiced at the healthy birth of their first child, Matthew, but less than a month later mourned the loss of her mother. At the time of her death, Catherine had 23 grandchildren, but Matthew, born in Ireland, was the only one she ever got to see. When Catherine bequeathed the farm to Martin, Margaret's brother James moved in with her and

Thomas, as discussed above. Over the next twenty years, six additional children followed. Margaret and Tom founded the McLoughlin branch of the family which still flourishes both in Ireland and the United States.

When contemplating the lives of these ten siblings, the question that inevitably comes to mind is: Did they make the right choices? There are other questions too. Did those who emigrated live better lives than they would have had if they had stayed at home? Did those at home do better once their siblings had sailed to America? The answers to these and other "What if..." musings come under what historians sometimes call "counter-factual history." We all indulge ourselves now and again in such thoughts in regard to large and small issues from the past, but recognize the futility of speculating on what might have been.

Still, it is legitimate to contemplate the choices and their consequences faced by this generation of McCormacks. First, it should be noted that all of those who left did so voluntarily. None left Ireland because of landlord eviction or government sponsored schemes to clear congested districts. In an era when many Irish considered themselves exiles from their native land, there is no evidence that any of the six siblings in America ever considered themselves unwilling refugees. They weighed their prospects at home and reached the reasonable conclusion that they had potentially brighter futures in America.

John, the eldest and first to leave, probably faced the hardest and most uncertain choice. Being first born was no guarantee of inheritance, and, as it turned out, John was 53 when the farm eventually changed hands. So, in his early 20s with no land and, hence, no real status as an adult, John faced bleak prospects at home. By then, emigration from Connacht was in full swing and letters from friends and acquaintances now in America arrived often in Frenchpark. As I speculated earlier, one of these letters, from his former neighbor, Peter Duignan, was probably instrumental in John's decision to leave home in 1886.

Once John was established in New Jersey, his brothers and sisters began to follow him. Fares were inexpensive, at least in terms of American wages, steamships were swift and safe, and every McCormack who made the crossing made emigration more appealing to their siblings. Four of the men came first, between 1886 and 1895, soon followed by two of their three younger sisters. There are no records or any McCormack family memory that the first arrivals sent pre-paid tickets home for their siblings. Nevertheless, that is likely to have been the case, as we know that the American siblings sent other money home and that vast amounts of money crossed the Atlantic to Ireland in these years in the form of remittances. In fact, a report from the Irish national schools in 1889 commenting of student writing exercises stated that "specimen letters inscribed by children ... were 'invariably written to some friend [abroad] asking the person to send a ticket to take them out.'"[46]

The McCormacks who left Ireland all fared well in America compared to their probable prospects at home. Patrick died young, but that might have been his fate in Frenchpark as well. Even after his death, his widow Delia never seems to have considered returning with their children to Ireland. In truth, by then, most of the family was here in America.

Did they make the right choice in coming to New Jersey? The answer depends on a number of considerations, not the least of which is how much one values economic success. It would be difficult to argue that the family in America was not economically better off than their siblings back home. While none of them rose above the working class, they all owned their own homes, and provided successfully for their children. At least two of them sent money and goods home to Ireland. There is no evidence that any of them thought that they had made a mistake by emigrating.

The McCormacks in Ireland lived much different lives. Three carried on the family farming tradition, while one entered British service in the RIC. Did they benefit from their siblings'

---

[46] Fitzpatrick, "Emigration," 615.

departure? Martin certainly had less competition for the farm when his brothers left, but that does not mean that he would not have inherited anyway. Margaret was able to receive a dowry and marry, but, again, she might have gotten it anyway. For William, it is difficult to speculate on any difference in prospects one way or the other due to siblings leaving. Still, for all those who remained in Ireland, the fewer there were of them, the less strain was put on the farm's resources, the less crowded was the small cottage. That had to count for something.

William McCormack Royal Irish Constabulary 1897

James McCormack 1944

Martin and Mary Ann McCormack at Farm 1951

Margaret McCormack McLoughlin, Granddaughter Mary and
Son Johnny McLoughlin 1953

Chapter 6
The Passing of the Torch

Pak was retired now, after 40 years working on the Rutland. All the children except Teddy had moved out, four were married, and Kate had five grandchildren. Fifty years married! Who could believe it? With the children gone, their little house seemed almost spacious, plus now there was even an indoor bathroom under the stairs, installed during necessary repairs after a recent fire caused by spilled kerosene. She and Pak were content; he would walk down to the village and come back with the groceries, Teddy would help around the house and Tom would stop by to see if they needed a ride anyplace. They had no car; never needed one. For that matter, they didn't have a telephone either. In good weather Kate spent much of her time in her rocking chair on the front porch, reading the paper, or sometimes just dozing.

Their visits to New Jersey had ended. John had died in '37 and Thomas the next year. Michael had passed on in '41. Her sisters-in-law were also gone; Helen had died young long ago, during the great flu epidemic in '18, Anne in '42, Annie in '48 and Pak's sister Delia's death in '47 had struck both of them very hard. Now there were just Kate and Bea in America and Martin and Margaret back home in Ireland. She put on her glasses and looked once more at the letter she had just received from Martin's wife Mary Ann:

Bea wrote just a few days ago that you would like to have a letter from home and that you had been sick lately. I hope that you will be alright when this letter reaches you. Where does the years go? I'm sure all your family is away from ye now; only yourself and Pak. Is he as nice to you as ever? I think of all the dear ones that's gone. R.I.P.. Martin is not feeling so well. For the last 12 months he has had to keep to the doctor. Lately his stomach bothers him a lot. God, he was proud when Bea said you would like to hear from home. He would love to have a letter from you... I am sending a shamrock to remind you of home.

Kate carefully folded the letter and put it in her apron pocket. I'll have to write home soon, she thought, as she drifted off to sleep in her rocking chair.

I began this project by seeking information about the twelve McCormacks in my grandmother's generation. I was fairly pleased with the results, though a number of them had left little behind beyond a very faint documentary trail. Some, like the first Patrick and his brother Thadeus, disappeared from history immediately after their baptisms, and others, in particular Michael, left few records and no one behind to remember them. Between 1890 and 1933 this generation produced 39 children in Ireland and America -- McCormacks, Callahans, Daniels, and McLoughlins. I now needed to investigate their lives as well.

Their parents had come of age in the late-19th century when rural Ireland was reeling from land disputes and declining agricultural prices while the United States was rapidly transforming into an industrial powerhouse. Irish society continued to operate within age-old traditions, while in America rapid change and innovation were everywhere. Arriving immigrants were stunned by the differences between America and home. Some lamented the loss of old communal ties; this is "a hard, merciless, self-seeking country" wrote one disillusioned immigrant.[1] Most, however, welcomed the change, as expressed in a column in the *Galway Vindicator in 1869*: [In America] "A man is a man if he's willing to toil."[2] The McCormacks in America took well to their new home, as evidenced by their continued arrivals between 1886 and 1903.

Unskilled labor and domestic service were the primary sources of employment for newly-arrived Irish immigrants in the late 19th century, and social mobility for the first generation of arrivals typically occurred within the working class.[3] The McCormacks fit this pattern well. Some had started their American careers as gardeners, coachmen or servants, but had

---

[1] Miller, *Emigrants and Exiles*, 477.

[2] Shrier, *Ireland*, 21.

[3] Kenny, *American Irish*, 149-50.

gone on to improve their lives as policemen or managing their own households. Only Michael seems to have remained in a lower level position. They had arrived poor, but they all owned their own homes before they died.

All of those who came to America married and had children, in contrast to their siblings who stayed behind where traditions regarding land holding and dowries limited one's marital choices. Kate married at 22, and Bea at 19, while their sister Margaret waited until she was nearly 30 to marry. Martin was in his mid-30s before he inherited the farm, wed and started his family. William, the policeman, had wed, but not until he was 40 and his bride was too old to have children. Yet even in Ireland in the early-20th Century conditions were changing dramatically. The next generation faced new challenges and opportunities. How did it fare?

The Second Generation and Historical Records

First, a word or two about historical records. The next generation of McCormacks in the United States began even before most of their aunts and uncles had left Frenchpark. I thought that discovering their history would prove much easier than had exploring the lives of their parents. After all, even though there were nearly four times as many of them, they lived more recently. People remembered them; some were even still alive. A quarter of their number were my own aunts and uncles. How hard could it be?

As a historian, I should have known better, and I soon did. At first, the historical records which had enabled me to delve into the lives of the first generation contained as well the basic vital statistics for their children. United States census returns for 1900, 1910, 1920 and 1930 chronicled the births, and sometimes revealed the deaths of all of the American branch of the family. Every decade I had the name of the head of the family, their spouse and their children. Though precise birthdates were not given in the census, I could estimate within a year when each of them was born. In some returns the census taker asked how many children had been born of the marriage and how many were still living. This information helped to reveal the certain deaths of children who otherwise would have simply disappeared from the historical record. One of Patrick and Delia's sons, Patrick Joseph, born in 1894, for example, had been alive in 1900, but dead by 1910. When, where or how he died are not yet known. But, had Delia not stated that four children had been born, but that only three were still living in 1910, Patrick Joseph's absence from the census could have simply meant that he had left home and gone to work, as he would have been 16 when the record was compiled. The census records also revealed where these cousins lived, some of their occupations, plus a couple of marriages as well. I was very fortunate that most of the McCormack descendants in New Jersey never strayed far from home.

These valuable records posed problems as well. The major drawback for American census records is that there is a mandated 72-year waiting period before they can be made public. This was implemented to protect the privacy of living citizens, but has a very negative impact on the work of historians and genealogists. So, just at the time when most of this generation were young adults, they become much more elusive. For the Irish side of the family, the problems with census records are even worse.

Under British rule, Ireland conducted census enumerations every ten years between 1821 and 1911. Of these, only the 1901 and 1911 records survive intact. Others were lost in fires, and the Anglo-Irish and subsequent civil wars. As mentioned above, the 1881 and 1891 returns, which would have been extremely valuable to trace the family's first generation, were deliberately pulped by the British government during World War I to alleviate a paper shortage. The problems in using the Irish census to reveal information about this second generation are, first of all, that no census was taken in 1921 because of the Anglo-Irish war, and the next census, in 1926, has not been released. In Ireland, as in the United States, there is a long waiting period before public release, in Ireland's case, a full century. So, the 1926 census, which would be extremely useful for this study, is not scheduled for release until 2027. There is hope, however, for an earlier release, as was done for both the 1901 and 1911 compilations. In short, then, there is no census information at this time to help with the history of the second generation of Irish McCormacks and McLoughlins, all of whom were born after 1911.

There are other restrictions as well on obtaining public records for this generation. The New Jersey State Archives, where I had obtained a number of birth, marriage and death records for both generations of the family only has birth statistics records up to 1923, marriages to 1940 and deaths to 1941. So, while I could get the birth records for almost all the second generation New Jersey McCormacks, most of their marriages and deaths records occurred after that date. The New Jersey Department of Health will provide later certificates if you have a legitimate right to them and if you already know the exact dates needed. New York State, where the Callahan records are filed, has the same 75 year waiting period for birth records and a 50 year period for marriage and death records. Fortunately, since the New York State branch of the family was the Callahans, I had my own sources of information.

I
The Second Generation in America

I decided to begin my research on the second generation at the beginning, with the family of John and Anne McCormick who had lived at 14 Llewellyn Avenue in West Orange. Their daughter, Winifred, born in May 1890 and named after Anne's mother, was the first child of this new generation. I came to know a good deal about her and the rest of John and Anne's family thanks to their granddaughter, Patty Davis, who had lived in the family home as a child and as an adult, had known many of her aunts and uncles, and remembered most of what she had ever learned about her ancestors. Since it stayed in the family for such a long time, the Llewellyn Avenue home had also become the repository for hundreds of family photos and other documents, all of which Patty preserved.

When she and her husband moved from Llewellyn Avenue to another family home in Bay Head, New Jersey in 1993 they took the archive along. Over the next few months I eagerly awaited Patty's e-mails that informed me she had found this photo or that diary in the attic or basement while looking for Christmas or other holiday decorations, or that she knew a particular photo or family Bible was around somewhere but that she hadn't found it yet. Eventually lists turned up to fill in many gaps in our knowledge of when McCormicks had been born or died, and photos brought images of people long dead to life again. There were even photographs of my grandparents visiting Patty's family, and her aunts, uncles and cousins visiting mine, proving that they had kept in contact. One photo I long thought contained images of my grandmother and her younger sister Bea was actually my grandmother and Patty's Aunt Anne McCormick.

The boxes also contained previously unknown 19th-century studio photographs of my grandmother as a teenager in Ireland, Martin as a young lad, three pictures of their mother, Catherine Keenan McCormack, and one of their brother William as a young RIC recruit. Others, such as those of Bea as a young domestic servant in Newark and later with her family, and of Michael and Helen on their wedding day demonstrated that the McCormacks both in Ireland and America had kept in touch in the late-19th and early-20th centuries. Duplicates were probably kept in the homes of John's siblings as well, but had been lost over time. The Americans undoubtedly also sent family pictures home. One of my Irish cousins said that there was once a photo of an American policeman on J. P. McCormack's mantel in Slieveroe. It was probably of John or Thomas, perhaps one that Thomas brought with him when he visited in 1931.

About a year after Winifred's birth, John bought the lot on Llewellyn Avenue where he built his house. Thus he became not only the first McCormick in America and the first to become a father, but also the first property owner. Anne was pregnant again at the time, and their second child, John, was probably born before the new house was completed. Baby John's life was cut tragically short when he died with convulsions from meningitis just over a year later. In October 1894 Anne gave birth to a second healthy daughter, Anne Beatrice, followed by two more sons and two more daughters, born about two years apart. Their last child, William Patrick, was born at the end of 1904.

All of John's children were raised on Llewellyn Avenue and stayed in West Orange all their lives. Two of the daughters, Winifred and Mary Rose, married and began their own families, while their sisters Anne Beatrice and Margaret Cecilia, remained single and at home. Compared to the family homestead in Ireland, John's house was quite large. There were four bedrooms upstairs and ample public space on the first floor. The two boys, Thomas S. and William P., shared an unheated enclosed porch as their bedroom. For most of the year that was an adventurous arrangement, but in the winter, ice often formed on the inside of the windows. At first there was no indoor bathroom, but that was not unusual in the early 20th century.

When she was 19, Winifred married Matthew O'Connell, an Irish immigrant of 29, who worked as a private chauffeur in West Orange. They lived with her parents for over a decade, eventually relocating to McKinley Avenue, not far away. Winifred became a full-time homemaker, raising five children. Her husband continued working as a chauffeur until the mid-1920s when he became a railroad policeman. In the early 1930s Matthew founded a trolley and bus line, called the Swamp Line, connecting to the Newark rail system.

Winifred's sister Mary Rose, born in 1899, married Robert Emmet Morrison from South Orange in the early 1920s. Robert was six years older and, like Mary, the child of Irish immigrants. Like his brother-in-law Matthew, he started his working life as a private chauffeur. The family lived on High Street in Orange where they raised their three sons, Richard, Robert, Jr. and John. After working as a stenographer before her marriage, Mary became a full-time homemaker, and Robert, in the 1950's and 1960s worked as a bus driver and handyman at the Beard School For Girls in Orange. Mary lived to be nearly 90, dying in May 1989.

Neither Anne Beatrice nor Margaret Cecilia ever wed. Anne, born in 1894, worked in business. She received a diploma from the Business Department of St. John's School in 1912 and was a stenographer early in her career. She then worked until retirement as the bookkeeper for the Newark Athletic Club. She died in October 1952. Margaret was never formally employed, but she enjoyed handicrafts, making among other items, blankets, dolls, doll clothes and ceramic ware. She died in 1964.

Of the sons, Thomas, born at the end of 1896, was the elder brother. Early on, he worked in the stock room at the Edison factory in West Orange, moving up to the position of foreman before following his father into the police force sometime before 1930 and later being promoted to sergeant. Thomas was twice a widower. His first wife, Barbara, died in 1927 after battling tuberculosis for two years. In 1929 Thomas married Loretta Samuelson Burns, a widow with two small children. Thomas and Loretta had one son, Thomas, and the family remained on Kling Street for the rest of her life. After Loretta's death, Thomas re-married for the last time to Mary Maguire and they moved to Elliott Place. He died in 1975 at age 78 after a routine surgical procedure went tragically wrong.

John and Anne's youngest child was William Patrick, born at the end of 1904, the last of the "Williams" of that generation in the American branch of the family. To help support the family, he began working at age 8, cleaning out the horse stalls for the local milkman before going to school. When he was 11, he wrapped parcels at the local A&P grocery. Three years later he became a stock boy at Edison Storage. In 1922 William completed a secretarial course at La Master Institute in East Orange and took a job as a secretary at Carnegie Steel in New York City, staying there for four years. During that time he attended New York University at night and received his CPA degree. From 1926 to 1930 he worked as a bookkeeper at Tiffany

Manufacturing Company. When the company re-located, William chose not to go, and borrowed money from his father to start his own business, a bold move as the Depression deepened across America. William, despite his education as an accountant, felt unsuited for office work and wanted a profession where he could work outdoors and deal with the public. He bought an Atlantic Richfield station, that later became an Esso franchise in the Ironbound section of Newark, which he operated for the next half century, through good times and bad. He remembered seeing people fleeing past the station in panic on Halloween Eve, 1938, the night of Orson Welles' radio broadcast of the frightening, but fictional, Martian landing in non-fictional Grover's Mill, New Jersey. William survived a number of stick-ups, including a violent robbery of his gas station in the late-1960s, but continued operating his business until late in life, even after suffering a slight stroke in 1977.

When his mother, Anne, died in 1942, William inherited the home on Llewellyn Avenue with the stipulation that his two maiden sisters, Anne and Margaret, be allowed to continue living there as well. This arrangement was perfectly suitable to him, as he had no intention of asking them to move. Five years later he married Rosemary Vukan, and started a family, which daughter Patricia, and son, William Jr., soon joined.

Soon after Patricia's birth William converted the house into a two family home by adding two new bedrooms, one up and one down, to the back of the house and adding a second kitchen upstairs. That way, William's family could live upstairs and his sisters would have the downstairs. Despite the now more formal physical separation, the family remained very close, with Patty often joining her aunts for breakfast before going off to school.

William P. was a Democrat and an ardent Irish nationalist, beliefs which were undoubtedly also those of his father John. He was proud of his Irish heritage, was a member of local Hibernian clubs, and was particularly upset that the newly independent Irish state had abandoned the banner depicting a harp on a green background for the tri-color green, white and orange flag. The latter flag had been around for over a hundred years, and had flown over the General Post Office during the 1916 Easter Rising, but had not been popular because many Irish, not just William, disapproved of the orange stripe. In many ways he was probably the most consciously "Irish" member of the second generation. He died at 79 on New Year's Day, 1984.

Of all of the McCormacks who settled in New Jersey, I was most interested in Patrick's and Delia's branch because, as I've mentioned, I was directly related to both of them. Surprisingly, they proved to be extremely difficult to track down. There was ample documentary evidence up to 1930, and it was a virtual certainty that descendants were still living. Cousins remembered seeing their son William A. They remembered William's children, Billy and Jeanne. They had lived down the street from them, or went to high school with them or had heard that Billy went to Seton Hall and had been a school teacher in Millburn. But, nobody had any idea where they were now. This is a phenomenon that I encountered often in my research, for the family had drifted far apart after the second generation, emotionally if not physically. So, the second cousins in the next generation, Grace, Jeanne, Patty, myself and many others, knew surprisingly little about their aunts' or uncles' families.

I began to do, as cousin Jeanne Lechner termed it, some sleuthing. I was sure that William A. and his wife were dead along with the rest of the members of that generation. What I needed to do was to find Billy or Jeanne who were older than I, but not that much older. Jeanne McCormack had been a year behind Jeanne Lechner in high school, when they were both Jeanne McCormack, probably causing much confusion. But, she had gotten married and no one knew her husband's name. Billy went to Seton Hall and had been, Patty thought, a teacher in Millburn, so possible avenues for investigation existed there. They both might have children, but no one knew for sure.

The crucial break came when I found William A.'s 1991 obituary in the *Newark Evening News* at the New Jersey State Library. It stated that he was survived by his wife, Mary Estelle, a daughter, Jeanne Fragetta, a son, William C., four

102

grandchildren and two great-grandchildren. So, I had now found Jeanne's married name and proof that the family had continued to another generation. A visit to the Social Security Death Index brought me the news that Mary Estelle had died three years later in 1994. Both had lived in West Caldwell at the time.

I checked various on-line telephone directories for the area, but could find no William McCormacks or Fragettas. Another check of the Social Security Death Index revealed some very bad news; Jeanne Fragetta had herself died in 2003. I noted that all three funerals had been held at the same funeral home, so I gave them a call in hopes that they could give me a contact number or address for living relatives. I was elated when the funeral director gave me the phone number for Jeanne's husband, William Fragetta, but when I called, I got the dreaded recorded message: "This number is no longer in service."

Next, I turned to a number of on-line "people finders" where one types in the name they're looking for and the location where they think they might be. I had no luck with William Fragetta, but got a couple of results for William C. McCormack. I had widened my search to all of New Jersey, but got the most promising hit from Florida. The search service I was using, called Private Eye, gives you a list of "possible relatives" and city locations for your subject. And, for a price you get a phone number as well as exact addresses. Since under "possible relatives" were listed "Estelle McCormack," and under addresses "McKinley Avenue in West Orange," I plunked down a few bucks and hit the jackpot. The only phone number that matched an actual address was for a William R. McCormack. I wrote on university letterhead so that even if I had the wrong person, I might get an answer. A few days later I got an e-mail stating "My name is William R. McCormack, grandson of William A. ... and would be happy to help."

He passed my e-mail address on to his mother Elena who also lives in Florida. From her I learned that William C. had also died a few years earlier. She was eager to help me and also put me in contact with her brother-in-law Bill Fragetta, who lives near Baltimore. From them I have received much valuable information on William A.'s family, plus some photographs, including one of Delia Callaghan McCormack. With their help, plus what I already knew about this branch of the family, I have been able to piece together at least the outline of its history.

--

Patrick and Delia's four children were born in the space of almost exactly four years between the start of 1893 and 1897. I have already discussed their early history above, from their moving to Pittsfield and Lebanon Springs after the tragic early death of their father, to the second son Patrick's death sometime between 1900 and 1910. When we pick up their story again they are back on Llewellyn Avenue where they started, right next door to their Uncle John. Delia was in a difficult position as a single mother before the advent of any government support or subsidies. As a young gardener, Patrick probably had no insurance, and he and Delia could hardly have saved much money in the six years they were married, especially with four young children. Still, in 1910, Delia owned #16 Llewellyn Avenue, though she had a mortgage.

The eldest son, Thomas M., was usually called Melvin. This was his grandmother's maiden name in Ireland, Magy Melvin. By age 17 he was helping to support the family by working as a driver for a dry goods store. In 1917, shortly after the United States entered World War I, he and his younger brother William A. went together to Newark and registered for the draft. Four months later, in early October, not waiting to be called up, Melvin traveled to New York City and enlisted in the Naval Reserve. There is a photograph of him wearing his new uniform in his back yard. He spent a month at the naval training camp at Pelham Bay Park in New York City. Here Melvin's story takes a strange turn. The only memory of him, passed down through his brother William's family, conflicts with the documentary record. Oral tradition in his family contends that he was gravely wounded in the war, leaving him with permanent injuries which led to his early death at age 36 in 1929.

The documentary record, however, shows that he never left the country. In fact, the farthest he got from New Jersey was the

Philadelphia naval yard.[4] According to his service record, a copy of which is filed in the New Jersey State Archives, Melvin went directly from the training camp to the naval hospital in New York where he spent three weeks for an unspecified illness. He was then sent to the 3rd Naval District Headquarters in New York where he spent the next nine months, finally being transferred to the Receiving Ship, a medical facility, in Philadelphia for inactive duty. He was discharged from there at the end of July 1919 and returned home.

What really happened with Melvin? It is difficult to be certain. Did he have an accident at training camp which made him unfit for active service? Where did the story of war injuries originate? He seems to have worked after his discharge, as both the 1920 census and his death certificate list his occupation as "office clerk." On his March 6th, 1929 death certificate, the cause of death is listed as "malnutrition occurring in depressed stage of Dementia Praecox." in other words, premature dementia.[5] In modern medical terminology it is a chronic disorder in which the mind deteriorates rapidly. At the time of Melvin's death it was often used interchangeably with schizophrenia. It is impossible now to determine exactly what mental disease he suffered from or when he began to exhibit symptoms, but it could well be that the early stage of this malady caused of Melvin's hospitalization and later discharge from the reserves. Perhaps in later years the fact that he was severely ill subsequent to his military service became conflated with the knowledge that many World War I veterans suffered debilitating injuries such as shell shock, resulting in the belief that the war had been the cause of his condition.

William A. McCormack, who accompanied Melvin to the draft board in 1917, had a much happier and longer life. He was not called for military service and continued his work as a clerk

---

[4] New Jersey State Archives, Adjutant General's Office (WWI), Unofficial Service Records, 1917, reel 36, "McCormack, Thomas Melvin."
[5] New Jersey State Archives, Death Register, Thomas M. McCormack, 9 March, 1929, Essex County, no. 25.

at Prudential Insurance's huge home office in Newark. He attended Pace University, receiving a degree in accounting. He continued his work at Prudential until 1923 when he began a nearly forty year career as an auditor for Edison Industries in West Orange. At the age when most people retired, William began a second career as an accountant for Paul Williams Inc. in Millburn, NJ, finally retiring at the age of 82 in 1978.

In August 1929 William married Mary Estelle Hayes, younger by ten years, of West Orange, and the couple lived with his mother Delia on McKinley Place, a two family house that served as both a home and investment property. Five years later they had their first child, Jeanne, given the middle name Melvin either after his grandmother or brother. In 1939, a second child, William C., followed. William and Mary remained in the family home after his mother's death in 1947 before moving to Orange and later to Caldwell. William A. was remembered fondly by not only his immediate family, but also by the other New Jersey McCormacks. His cousin Jeanne Lechner recalls that he was her godfather and always sent her a dollar on her birthday, and Patty Davis remarked that when you talked with him he always gave you his full attention, even though you were just a kid. William died in 1991 at the age of 95, followed three years later by his wife of 62 years, Mary Estelle.

The last of Patrick and Delia's children was Mary Agnes, sometimes known as Mollie, born in 1897. Not much is known about Mollie beyond the facts that she worked as a stenographer in a real estate office for a while and then as a secretary for an executive at a major paint company. When her boss was transferred to Kentucky she went along in some capacity. There was also some sort of family estrangement between Mollie and her brother, probably stemming from Delia's last years. There is a family story that Delia suffered from Alzheimer's at the end of her life at the time when Mollie left for Kentucky, leaving William and Mary Estelle to care for her on their own. Understandably, this left some hard feelings, and Mollie and William A. avoided contact afterwards. She returned to New

Jersey after retirement and lived out her life at a Catholic Institution in Morris County

--

Thomas and Annie had only one child, William J. McCormack, and I already knew his two daughters, Grace and Jeanne. So, compared with the difficulties of finding information about William A. and his siblings, researching William J. was going to be easy. William was born in July 1902. In a series of letters to his grandchildren when he was around 80 he wrote about his early life, how his mother had wanted him to become a violinist, "...but I was just a flat fiddler who would love to be playing ball in the street when I had to practice, and I wasn't any good on the violin. The dog ... knew that I couldn't play the violin; he ... would put his nose under the kitchen table and howl."[6] She also thought it would be nice for him to become a priest, but, as he recalled, "The Lord did not want me in the priesthood. I think I really would have upset the church."[7] One other memory from his youth was that when he was young he started to throw balls with his left hand and "...my good old Irish mother was horrified. She said I was a kithouge [Irish slang for left-hander] which was to her as bad as being a Lutheran."[8] In another particularly sweet note to the children about what grandfathers are he wrote:

Some...[like me] remember when automobiles ran on dirt roads and had funny horns on the outside and when we never saw airplanes, let alone traveled in them. Families rode in trolley cars and only the very wealthy owned an automobile. We did not have oil heat, but coal burning furnaces, and there were ashes to put out. Neither radio nor television was invented and very few people had telephones. Yet, we were very happy. ... My grandfathers lived in Ireland. I never saw them. I am

---

[6] Letter, William J. McCormack to grandchildren, 18 May, 1978. Collection of Jeanne Lechner.
[7] Ibid.
[8] Ibid.

glad that Newark, Delaware [where his grandchildren lived] is not as far away as Ireland...[9]

William J. graduated in a class of 33 from St. Benedict's Preparatory School in Newark, and worked for a year at a bank. He then enrolled in Rutgers Law School and received his law degree in 1925. He entered private practice in Orange. Over the next decades he was president of the Orange Bar Association for five terms and taught law at Fordham University in New York. William was active in politics as well, and an ardent Democrat. He was party chairman for a while in West Orange, and ran for the General Assembly in the 1930s – and lost. While practicing law for over a half century William J. also held a number of positions in New Jersey state government. He was an assistant attorney general between 1934 and 1944, and ten years later began a twenty year association with the State Department of Transportation. He began as a counsel for the department in 1954 and served as the chief counsel from 1956 to 1973. One of the highlights of this period was when he served as one of the two state attorneys who acquired title to the Meadowlands in Hackensack for the state.

In 1929 William married Loretta Vreeland from Orange and the couple moved to the house on Dartmouth Road where their daughter Grace still lives. In 1974 he left his position at the Transportation Department and returned to a limited private practice until his death in 1984.

--

Michael and Helen's three children left little behind besides basic vital statistics information. Only the eldest, Mary A., born in 1902, left any record of employment. Both the 1920 and 1930 census returns list her as a typist and bookkeeper, the latter return adds for an un-named grocery corporation. After that she disappears from records until 1941 when she was the informant on her father's death certificate. Her sister Catherine, a year younger, has no recorded employment. She lived into old age at

---

[9] Letter, William J. McCormack to grandchildren, 28 July 1980. Collection of Jeanne Lechner.

the family home on Ashland Avenue in West Orange. Cousins recall seeing her at family gatherings and receiving holiday cards from her up until her death, shortly before 1980. The youngest child, John, born in 1906, is a particular mystery. In the 1930 census under occupation is listed simply "none" with the addition of "sick." What he was sick with, no one now knows. In 1944, at the age of 38 he died at home of an unknown acute intestinal blockage. No autopsy was performed.

Michael's family is thus the least known branch of the McCormacks. The main reason for this, of course, is that none of his children married and had offspring. Whatever was known about the family perished when the last of his offspring died. Even the house they lived in no longer exists.

--

The other extreme is my grandmother's family, about which I know a good deal. Unlike her brother John's family, which remained local to West Orange in the next generation, most of Catherine's children left their hometown as soon as they could. This difference in settlement patterns is due for the most part to the fact that West Orange, NJ and Chatham, NY were very different places. Unlike West Orange, which had numerous employment opportunities, including the Edison factory, Chatham was, and still is, a small village surrounded by farms. It was originally Chatham 4 Corners, revealing its main reason to exist: it was a convenient crossroads for travelers headed up the Hudson valley and points east and west. When the railroads arrived in the mid-19th century, Chatham became the northern terminus of the Harlem Division of the New York Central, the southern terminus of the Rutland and the western terminus of the Boston and Albany. It was a railroad town and not much else. There were no other real industries to provide employment. A patent medicine, "Vegetable Cancer Cure" had sold well for a short time at the turn of the century, but the manufacturer never employed many people. There was a small shirt factory which provided jobs to a few women, and there were the farms. In West Orange, the police force beckoned not only to Catherine's brothers John and Thomas, but also to one of John's sons. The police force in Chatham consisted of only two men, the chief and one part-time patrolman. So, for Kate and Pak's children it was basically work on the railroad or leave town.

Most chose to leave. Of their nine children only two stayed in Chatham: my father, who worked on the railroad, and his youngest brother, Ted, who by the time he went to work had a new option, the power company. The rest scattered around the eastern United States, some to predictable places.

This was the case with the eldest child, Madeline, born in 1900. She lived at home until she was at least 20 and then moved to Newark, NJ to begin work as a clerk at the Prudential Insurance Company. For most young women in the small upstate village such a move would have been quite surprising, but Madeline already had a strong connection to New Jersey, through both her father's and mother's families. In fact, her first cousin, William A. McCormack, was working at Prudential at the time. It is quite likely that he suggested the move, and perhaps even helped her get the job. She spent her entire career at Prudential, being promoted by 1941 to Correspondence Administrator, a position she held until her retirement in 1965.

Madeline never married and lived most of her life with her younger sister Mary, who had moved to Newark as well by 1930. She would come back to Chatham each year for Christmas to join the family gathering. Her last years were spent at a nursing home in West Orange, where she died at age 78 in 1978.

Kate and Pak's second child was yet another William – William John Callahan, born in 1903. Early on, he stopped using his first name and became simply John Callahan. When he was barely 16 he went to work as a fireman on the Rutland, shoveling coal into the fireboxes on steam engines. He lived at home contributing to family support until 1928, when he married Cora Mohan from Brandon, Vermont, whom he had probably met in the course of his work, as the Rutland had a station in her town. By that year William had been promoted to section foreman, like his father Patrick. By 1930 the couple had re-located farther up the line to Brainard, NY, where they rented a modest apartment.

In the census that year, William had reversed his first and middle names to become "John William."

Of all my Callahan aunts and uncles he is the one I know least about. He and Cora had two daughters, Jean and Anne, and although Cora kept close contact with the family over the years, we seldom saw John. They and their children moved to Malone, NY, near the Canadian border where he, I think, continued to work for the railroad. He died from a heart attack at the age of 61 in 1964. I cannot recall ever meeting his daughters, though there is a snapshot from 1948 that proves I did. As evidence to the lack of family closeness among the Callahans, I have no idea where these cousins are, or even if they are still alive. Neither of my other first cousins has any knowledge of their whereabouts either. Jean apparently stayed close to her Aunt Mary, but not to most of the rest of the family. I recently found a 1998 Vermont death record for Cora where the informant was her daughter Jean, but a letter sent to the address given was returned as undeliverable by the post office.

The Callahan who moved farthest from home was the second son, Augustine, born in 1905. He left home as a teenager to work on a farm in Morristown in northern New Jersey. There he met Evelyn Gardner and the couple wed in 1925 when Augustine, or Auggie as he was known in the family, was 20 and she was 17. The next year their only child, a daughter named Ida, was born. For the next few years Auggie continued to work on the large farm, soon becoming the superintendent controlling its day-to-day management. Eventually, however, he trained as an electrician and worked for various power companies. The family permanently relocated to northern Florida in 1952, where Auggie retired.

I had never met Auggie or any of his family until the mid-1970s when I happened to be in St. Augustine. He had not returned to Chatham for several decades, and our contact with him had always been those awkward telephone calls announcing a family death. I checked the phone book at the hotel, called, and was invited over to his home. When I pulled up out front a man, looking remarkably like my father, stepped out on the porch and greeted me. We had a wonderful visit during which I also met his wife, Evelyn, daughter Ida and her husband, Lacey McCumber. A couple of years later I saw in the newspaper that Ida's son Mark McCumber had won his first professional golf tournament and had told reporters that some of his winnings were going to buy his grandparents a new car. Some time later, in 1981, we got a call that Auggie had died. My father took the news hard for he and his brother, though far apart geographically, were close in age and had always seen eye to eye on family matters. They were both dismayed when my maiden aunts routinely refused to do what needed doing in settling family estates – wills were not a family forte – because, they said, someone in the family "might want the property" some day. My father often referred to Auggie as the "smart one" in the family for getting far away from Chatham as soon as possible.

The next of Kate's children, the one without whom this present study would not be happening, was my father, Thomas Callahan, born in 1907. He remembered as a young boy helping around the house in Lebanon Springs, going up to pay the rent to the Shakers, as mentioned earlier, and helping to cut and store ice in the winter. When his father came home from work he would sometimes give Tom a dime and send him up to the bar a half mile or so away to get a small bucket of beer – as it was called at the time, "rushing the growler." My father could keep the two cents change and buy himself an ice cream cone.

In 1918, when he was 11, the family moved to Chatham. Tom left school after eighth grade to go to work to help support the family. One of his first jobs, at 14, was as a delivery boy for Hess' Market, where he got to drive the Ford Model T delivery truck. When he was old enough, his father got him a job on the Rutland, and by 1929 he had left to work as a brakeman on the New York Central. He spent 25 years there, becoming a conductor by the mid-1930s. He tried to volunteer for service in World War II, but was rejected because his current railroad job was deemed essential war work.

In the late-1930s he met and began to court Evelyn Colby, 10 years his junior, whose father also worked for the New York

Central. It was a long courtship, but they finally married in 1944, and I came along a year later. By the early 1950s Tom had begun to have some nagging health problems which he attributed to his railroad work, so he took a medical leave which effectively turned into early retirement. He may have been right about the cause of his maladies, because his health returned to normal shortly afterwards. While on the railroad he had begun to work part-time as a gunsmith as well, and now that became his full-time career. He opened a shop in the basement of our home and operated it for nearly 30 years. He was also active in the fire department and local politics, serving a term as mayor of Chatham – a time I loved because I got to ride in the police car as an 8-year old – and later as town clerk. He spent his last years in the New York State Firemen's Home in Hudson, suffering from diabetes and other disabilities. He died there at 85 in 1993.

I am not sure why he stayed in Chatham while most of his siblings left. I never asked him. In part, of course, it was due to his early work on the railroad, but, like John, he could have done that elsewhere. Meeting and marrying a local Chatham girl was also a factor. His work during the war also limited other options. I think, however, that he particularly felt an obligation to look after his parents, a responsibility that increased with each year he stayed and with each sibling who left. He fulfilled that commitment well, though he frequently grumbled about being "stuck with" this or that unpleasant task. For me, it was a boon I did not recognize at the time: I got to know my grandparents better than did any of my cousins.

Two years after my father, in 1909, the "mystery man" in our branch of the family was born, Andrew Callahan. All his surviving photographs show a small, wiry, handsome man, and had you met him in person you would be struck by his bright red, curly hair which he had clearly inherited from his mother. We don't know much about his early life, nor his later one. He appears in both the 1910 and 1920 censuses as a child and in 1930, still living at home and unemployed. He was a noted athlete in high school and held a number of jobs as a young man, including as a crossing guard for the Rutland Railroad in

Chatham. In 1934 he won $400 from the *Chatham Courier* in a contest to get new subscribers. Just before World War II he had apparently followed his brothers in choosing a railroading career, as his military enlistment records note that he was a "skilled railroad switchman" on his enlistment at the end of January, 1942. So, naturally, the army used him as a mail clerk during the war. He served in the Luzon, New Guinea and Southern Philippines campaigns, and was sent to occupied Japan at the war's end. During the war he wrote home as often as he could and sent back a large number of souvenirs, including wads of Japanese "occupation money" and, somehow, an entire set of equipment for a Japanese soldier – uniform, boots, underwear, rifle and samurai sword! They were a big hit in little Chatham in 1944.

He was discharged at Fort Dix, New Jersey in November 1945 and returned home briefly before moving to Newark. He was my favorite uncle, in part because I never saw the others much, except Uncle Ted, who was not nearly as dashing. I was always thrilled when he showed up at my grandparents' house for Christmas. He'd kid around with me and tell me war stories, and gave me a photo of himself in uniform somewhere in the Pacific with a parrot on his shoulder. Then one day when I was 10 a phone call came from my aunts in Newark that Andy was dead. He was 46. I still do not know what happened to him. My parents were always very vague in their explanation, as if they didn't want to tell me the truth, and yet didn't want to outright lie. I had heard that he was a railroad detective, but that hardly seemed a very dangerous job. In later years my older cousins have told me that they never got a straight story either.

Two years after Andy's birth, at the end of November, 1911, Mary Veronica Callahan was born. Like her elder brother she too had bright red hair, and was quite a beauty in her youth. We know nothing much at all about her early life, though a number of school photos survive and I still have her Arbor Day garden trowel painted in the colors of her class. In 1930, she was in Newark working as a sales clerk at Western Electric and living with her sister Madeline, an arrangement that continued for the rest of their lives. I am certain that they kept in touch with their New Jersey cousins, but I have no evidence for this belief. By 1940 Madeline had helped her get a job with her at Prudential Insurance, and she was an office supervisor there until her retirement in the mid-1970s. At one point she was sent to Florida to set up a new office and got to visit a while with her brother Auggie. After Madeline's death in 1978 Mary, never the healthiest of the siblings, deteriorated rapidly, dying in early 1979.

I did not know her very well, even though I was nearly 40 when she died. She was the sort of aunt who was always wanting hugs and kisses which put me off when I was a child. It didn't help that she smoked incessantly. After my grandparents' deaths in the 1950s I saw her only twice, both times at funerals, my Uncle Ted's in 1969 and my mother's in 1975.

In 1914 Robert Emmet Callahan was born. Like Robert Emmet Morrison, Mary Rose McCormick's husband in New Jersey, he was named after an early martyr for Irish independence, Robert Emmet, who was hanged, drawn and quartered by the English in Dublin in 1803. If nothing else, this choice of names betrays my grandparents' political sympathies. They must have been transfixed by the Easter Rising two years after his birth. Robert graduated from Chatham High School and went to work in a Chatham shoe store. He soon met Mary Cook, a fifth grade teacher there and they married in September 1937. They honeymooned in New York and Newark, where they undoubtedly called on relatives. Though they had apparently planned to stay in Chatham, they left soon after the birth of their only child, James William, in 1940, and relocated near Waterloo, NY. where Robert managed a number of shoe stores. On the weekend after Thanksgiving in 1962 Robert was killed in an automobile accident near home.

The youngest son, Timothy, known as Ted, was born at the beginning of 1919, the first of the siblings to be born after the move to Chatham. He was a star athlete in high school, graduating in 1937. What he did immediately after graduation is unknown, but he continued to live at home. In early 1941 with World War II already underway in Europe, Ted enlisted in the army and served as a private first class after the United States entered the war at the end of the year. Following the D-Day invasion in 1944 Ted participated in the European theatre, serving first in southern France where he was awarded the Combat Infantry Badge. Wounded at the Battle of the Bulge, he was hospitalized briefly in France before being sent back to the United States. He was eventually discharged at Fort Dix New Jersey in October, 1945.

What he did for the next few years is also unknown. In 1949 he began working on the line crew of New York Electric and Gas Corporation where he remained for twenty years. In late 1968 he was diagnosed with intestinal cancer already too far advanced for any hope of a cure. He died at the Veterans Administration hospital in Albany almost exactly fifty years after his birth.

He lived in his parents' house all his life, for the last twelve years by himself. Despite the fact that we lived in the same small village I never knew him very well. I cannot recall him ever coming to our house for dinner, on holidays or even just to stop by. He never owned a car, but we lived less than a mile away. For that matter, I cannot recall ever going to my grandparent's house again after they died, until Ted's death. When my father and I went to see what needed to be done we found the house a shambles. One thing in particular stood out. Ted had no washer or dryer, so instead of going down to the laundromat in town he simply wore his clothes until they were too dirty, threw them into one of the spare bedrooms and bought new clothes. My father took one look at the house and ordered a dumpster.

The last of Catherine's nine children, Eleanor, was born in 1921 when Kate was 45. Eleanor's early life is pretty much a blank. There are a few childhood photographs plus a listing of her name at age 9 on the 1930 census. There are also a series of snapshots of her posing with McCormick relatives visiting from New Jersey around 1940, but that's about it. She attended college after high school – the first Callahan to do so. Her first documentary appearance after college is a teacher's contract between her and the Morristown Board of Education in St. Lawrence County NY on the Canadian border for the 1942-43 school year. For forty weeks teaching Eleanor was paid the munificent total of $880.00.[10] We do not know what she taught, but it was probably French, for that was her subject area in later years. Some time later she moved down the St. Lawrence to Fort Covington where she spent the rest of her career. She, like her sisters, never married. We would see her at Christmas until her parents died and get cards or phone calls on holidays and birthdays, but knew little else about her.

It seems strange that I know more about relatives long dead that I never met or even knew existed than I do about most of my aunts and uncles. My Callahan cousins and I joke about how the family isn't "close" when every few years we feel the urge to contact each other. The best way to describe the family dynamic now is not estrangement, but simple apathy.

This might also be the situation with the family of Bridget [Bea] McCormack Daniels, the last of the siblings to arrive in America. Bea and her husband Ernest had three children, two sons and a daughter. The eldest, Ernest William, was born at the beginning of 1911. In the 1930 census, Ernest was working as an auto supply clerk. He then disappears from the written record, except for a possible listing in the Social Security Death Index in 1992. There is, however, an intriguing family photograph, probably from the early 1940s, of Ernest and his family – his wife Frances and daughters Dianne, Patricia and Eileen, who range in age from about five years to a few months. I have been unable to find anyone who knows anything about any of these people, except that they lived in New Jersey. Various other searches have also

---

[10] Teacher's contract, Board of Education, Morristown, St. Lawrence County, NY and Eleanor Callahan, 17 August 1942. Collection of author.

turned up nothing. If the daughters are now married, there's no way of knowing what their married names are.

Ernest's younger brother, William Joseph, was born in 1914. We know nothing about his childhood beyond his listing in the 1920 and 1930 census as a student. We also know nothing about him as an adult except from a photograph taken during World War II which shows him in uniform standing outdoors next to his wife Mary Brady. According to the Social Security Death Index he died in 1974.

Bea and Ernest's last child, a daughter they named Mary Elizabeth, was born in 1920. Shortly after the beginning of World War II she married Harry Franklin, and in September 1944 their daughter Anita was born. Tragically, Harry was killed in the war, and Bea helped her daughter raise Anita. Mary wed again to Eugene Prococco and they had four children. We know nothing more about her beyond a few photographs taken with the McLoughlin branch of the family and a mass card attesting to her death in 1970.

--

The six McCormack siblings who emigrated to the United States had a total of twenty-seven children, twenty-five of whom survived to adulthood. It is reasonable to claim that all of those who came from Ireland fared better here than if they had stayed at home. None of the four brothers would have inherited the farm, and neither of the women would have been provided a dowry for marriage. Evidence indicates that they were all literate when they arrived. They were the products of the Irish national education system which had been in operation since their parents' time and which taught basic skills in reading, writing and arithmetic as well as offering some training in farm management for boys and sewing for girls. Small district schools were scattered around the country, run either by the Protestant or Catholic clergy, depending on where they were located. Since most of the students were the children of farmers and often needed to work at home, daily attendance averaged only slightly over 40% in most years in the late-19th century.[11] Still the results were impressive and parents were serious about sending their children as often as possible. This was especially true for those who would be emigrating. Irish parents knew that literacy in English was essential in America.

None of the first arrivals had any sort of advanced education, and the jobs they held required none. All of the men began in laboring or servant positions, two as gardeners and two as coachmen, or drivers. After a few years in New Jersey, John, Thomas and Michael moved on to other work, while Patrick died young, still working as a gardener. John and Thomas joined the police force, clearly a step up from gardening and driving, while Michael made more of a lateral move from a coachman to a janitor at a Catholic parochial school. It is interesting to note that none of them, though they came from a farming background, expressed the slightest interest in becoming farmers in America. This is unremarkable, however, since a miniscule percentage of the American Irish became farmers, especially those who stayed on the east coast. Historians have speculated that if rural emigrants' Irish experiences convinced them of anything, it was that farming was not the way to get ahead.

The two sisters, Kate and Bridget, became homemakers and raised their children. So far as we know, Kate never worked for a wage outside the home. Bridget, however, began her life in America as a maid for a number of years before starting her own family. Had they remained at home, it is likely that neither of them would have been able to marry.

The next generation of McCormacks in the United States fared even better. Of the twenty-five children who survived to adulthood, fourteen were male and eleven female. All of them got at least an 8th grade education, at which point some left school and got jobs to help with family finances. That was the case with at least two of Kate's children, my father and his brother John, both of whom went to work when they were

---

[11] D. Atkenson, *The Irish Education Experiment* (Toronto: University of Toronto Press, 1970), 321.

fourteen or fifteen. It is likely that there were others as well, especially among the males, but I do not know. The rest graduated from high school, either public or parochial, and framed certificates and diplomas show that their parents were extremely proud of them. A few received some form of higher education. In the Callahan branch, only one, Eleanor, went to college. Among the McCormacks and McCormicks, two, William A. and William P., became certified public accountants and one, William J., a lawyer. It was not until the next generation, which is beyond the scope of the present study, that higher education became widespread, a phenomenon which was normal for these times in the United States.

Most members of this second generation were employed outside the home at some point during their lives. None of the women who married were employed after marriage, though one worked as a stenographer before her wedding. Two of the unmarried women left no record of employment, but the others all supported themselves with full-time jobs, ranging from secretarial work to office management and teaching positions. Only one of the males who reached adulthood has no recorded employment, and he is listed in the relevant column of the 1930 federal census as "none, sick." The others held a wide range of jobs, some at entry or unskilled level, but most of which were better than the jobs their fathers had. Three of Kate's sons, for example, worked on the railroad as had her husband Patrick, but all of them at a higher level. There were two certified public accountants, a lawyer who worked in the top levels of state government, and two who owned their own businesses. Almost all members of this generation lived what one would term middle class lifestyles, though most were technically in working class positions. As was the case above with education, the next generation would prosper even more with scientists, teachers, lawyers, managers and medical professionals.

When one looks at rate of marriage in the second generation a curious picture emerges. Only half of them ever married, and when the numbers are considered by gender, the resulting numbers are even more unbalanced. Ten of the fourteen males married, but only three of the eleven females. Why did so few wed when men did not need property to marry and women married without any expectation of a dowry?

Like most Irish-Americans of their generation, the McCormack descendants supported Irish nationalism and considered their parents to have been exiles who had to leave Ireland because of British oppression. They inherited the spirit that had led their parents to name sons "Robert Emmet" and to despise the English. I do not know what my grandmother thought of the British, but her husband Pak denounced them roundly. My father used to needle him at times, reminding him that he had lived in England briefly before emigrating and liked the English family he boarded with. My grandfather simply responded "They were different."

This pugnacious attitude sometimes carried over into dealings with American authorities. In 1961, for example, William P. McCormick, frustrated by continued bills from the City of Newark for water service that his gas station never received, sent a letter of complaint to the city Director of Finance which concluded:

> Well, Sir, the reason my ancestors came and settled in the good old United States of America is because they did not like to live in a foreign land under threats and tyranny, and I intend to carry out their tradition by not living under the threat of some imbecilic head of a water department who is having meters read THAT DO NOT EXIST and who is going to shut off water valves that have been shut off for six years....Thank you![12]

We do not know if the problem was rectified, but I suspect that it was.

---

[12] William P. McCormick, letter to Mr. Schorn, Newark Department of Finance, 16 January 1961. Collection of P. Davis.

II
The Second Generation in Ireland

The second generation in Ireland, though fewer in numbers, proved more elusive to trace. A major difficulty concerns official records, in particular, census records. For the American McCormacks I had annual census surveys for every decade from 1900 to 1940, plus easy access to birth and marriage records at the New Jersey State Archives. In Ireland, however, as I discussed above, the only available 20th century census tallies are from 1901 and 1911, both of which pre-date the births of any of the twelve members of this generation. There was no census taken in 1921, due to the Anglo-Irish War, and the first subsequent survey, 1926, has not yet been released. In addition, though civil birth, marriage and death records have been kept since 1864, their completeness is spotty and patrons are not allowed go to the Registry Office and browse through the holdings to find relevant documents. Consequently, I have had to rely heavily on family memories, cemetery inscriptions and ephemera such as mass cards.

Three of the four siblings who remained in Ireland married, and two had children. The first of these was Martin, the youngest son who inherited the family farm when his mother Catherine died in 1915. His and Mary Ann's first child, Ellie Kate, died as an infant and is buried in an unmarked graveyard in Sheepwalk, just outside Frenchpark, where the Into The West pub is now located. She is buried there because she died before being baptized, so could not be interred in consecrated ground. Sister Joseph remembers a baby from her family also being interred there when she was young.

This practice of using an "unofficial" cemetery certainly seems odd to us today, but was common several decades ago. While it was unmarked, the graveyard was not a secret. Though no one spoke about the burials, everyone knew they had taken place, and nothing was ever planted on the land. About a decade ago there was a special Mass conducted at the field by Fr. Early, the parish priest in Frenchpark, who finally blessed the ground. A simple stone monument reading "Blessed Are The Meek For They Will Inherit The Earth" was placed there in 2003.

Their second child, Mary Jane, better known as Mai, was born in September 1921. She recalls a happy youth growing up on the farm with her brothers and sisters. As I have said, she has a wonderful memory. She vividly remembers the visits of her father's brother and sister over 80 years ago, including even the first name of Madge Callaghan Sharkey who traveled with my grandmother. When I asked her about her education at the nearby Cloonmagunane National School when she was a child, she said that she and her classmates were taught Irish, but added "Little good it did."[13] She also said that the children were expected to bring a piece of turf to school with them in cold weather to help with heating the building. She told me that the family never had a car, but got around with a pony trap, a small, two-wheeled cart pulled by a pony. One day Mai's father had an errand to run near Fairymount. But, unaccountably, the pony stopped on its own in front of several cottages along the way. Telling his family about this on his return, he learned that his wife, when she went to Fairymount, would always stop to visit with her many friends and relatives. The pony knew the route as well as she did.

During the Second World War, after she finished national school, Mai departed in 1943 for nursing school in England and her younger sister Margaret, born in June 1923, followed a year later. Mai had wanted to be a nurse since she was about 9, and she thinks that Margaret chose nursing because of her. During the war there was a desperate need for nurses in England because of mounting casualties. Consequently, the British government offered free nursing education, while Ireland did not. Mai says that there was no way she or Margaret could have afforded the tuition at home, so they left. Mai stayed in England, working most of her career at Mary Dendy Hospital in Cheshire. She married an Englishman, Arnold Robinson, in 1959, and they

---

[13] Interview with Mai Robinson 12 May 2010.

123

had one son, Timothy. Mai, now widowed, is retired and lives with her son near London.

Her sister Margaret, as mentioned above, also trained as a nurse. She remained in England for a while, working as a mental health nurse, but later returned home and married Michael Carty from nearby Ratra in 1958, and they had two sons. She died in 1978.

The next three children remained near the family homestead. The first son, John P., was the man Ellen and I met in 1982. He was born in 1924, and inherited the farm when his mother died in 1962. Under his stewardship the size of the farm nearly doubled with the purchase of nine additional acres. He never married, and when he died in 2001 the farm passed to his nephew, James Dowd.

J. P.'s younger sister, Bridget Theresa, known as Beatie, was born in June, 1927 and trained as a teacher in England. After a short teaching career she returned to Frenchpark and married a local farmer, Tim Dowd, in 1952. They had six children, all of whom still live in Ireland. Her sons, John and James, now farm both their parents' land and the family homestead. Beatie had written to me in 2003, informing me of her brother's death, and we exchanged holiday cards until her death from cancer in 2005.

The story of the youngest son, Willie – William Joseph – is a sad one. He was born in 1928 during my grandmother's visit home. In fact, they shared a birthday, 11 December. My grandmother was one of the sponsors at his christening before she returned home. In 1949, when Willie was 21, his mother wrote to Kate: "Willie Joe, the one Kate you stood for, is big, he must be nearly 6 foot tall, a real McCormack. Bea has told us she would try and get him out to the USA after a while... Indeed there is nothing here for anyone, the times is looking very bad at the present."[14]

Emigration was not to be, however, as Willie was found dead in bed one morning two years later when J. P. went to wake him

---

[14] Letter from Mary Ann McCormack to Catherine Callahan, 7 March 1949. Collection of author.

to go cut turf. Mai remembers that she and her sister Margaret had just returned to England after a visit home to see their father who was very ill when a telegram arrived summoning them back. They thought that Martin had died and were stunned to find instead that it was their little brother. He had died on 22 March 1951 when a blood vessel burst in his brain. The next few days were grim. A wake for Willie was held at the house, but Martin, just in the next room, was too ill to attend. Mai recalled: "Father never saw him dead."[15]

--

The youngest McCormack sibling, Margaret, had one baby buried in the unmarked graveyard and seven children who survived. The eldest, Matthew, born in 1915, became a priest. His uncle William, formerly with the RIC, paid for Matthew's education at the seminary in Maynooth. Fr. Matt, as he was known in the family, spent part of his career in Strokestown, where the Famine Museum is currently located, and his last parish was in Sligo. He also spent time visiting relatives, both McCormacks and McLoughlins, in New Jersey over the years, as he appears in a large number of snapshots from various family branches. Margaret Stefanelli, a niece, recalls him presiding over mass in the back room of her father's bar in West Orange. He died in 2000 on his 85th birthday.

A daughter Katie was born two years after Matthew, in November 1917. As a young woman she moved to Newry in County Down in Northern Ireland where she worked as a draper's assistant. While there, she continued courting John Reynolds, whom she had met earlier in Ballaghdereen. John had subsequently moved to Dublin to work in his uncle's pub, and there, in April, 1942, and she and John married. Following their marriage, the couple relocated to England where he worked first as a laborer and later as a foreman on a number of projects. At one point Katie worked as the manager of one of the work camp canteens. Over the years Katie and John had three children, two boys and a girl, and bought a house in Poole, Dorset, where they

---

[15] Interview with Mai Robinson, 13 May 2010.

remained. In Poole Katie worked as a cleaner at the hospital and rented out rooms to young nurses. Eventually she and her husband sold the house and moved to a senior citizen housing complex. John died in 1999 and Katie passed on at age 93 after a long illness in July 2010.

The next son, John, was born in 1919, inherited the family property when his parents died and farmed in Callow. In 1951 he married Ellie Noon, a local woman who had trained as a nurse in England and later worked as a matron in a boy's boarding school. They had seven children, one of whom died a month after his birth. One of their sons, Tom, his wife Ann and their family now live in the family homeplace, which has been much expanded. John died in 1982.

There's an old saying that every Irish family should have a priest or nun, and the McLoughlins have both. The next daughter, Bridget, now known as Sr. Joseph, born at the end of 1922, became a nun at Our Lady of the Missions in 1939. Though she came to the United States only once, as she can be found in numerous American photographs. She is currently retired and living in Dublin, and frequently visits her childhood home. She remarked during a recent dinner in the expansive dining/family room, "This used to be our turnip patch."[16]

Margaret and Thomas' 5th child was Maggie, born in 1925. She trained as a nurse in England, married John Allen in England, and lived there all her life. John and Maggie had three children.

The last two of Margaret and Tom's children emigrated to the United States after World War II. The first of these was Patrick, better known as Paddy McLoughlin, born in May 1927. Like his siblings, he had grown up on the farm and, as a teenager, devoted much time and effort caring for his ailing Uncle James at the end of his life. After James' death, Paddy had enlisted in the Irish Army Reserves and became a truck driver, but realized that his future in Ireland was limited because his older brother John was slated to inherit the family farm. So at the end of 1947 Patrick applied at the American consulate in Dublin for

---

[16] Interview with Sr. Joseph McLoughlin, May 15, 2011.

permission to emigrate to the United States.[17] This act itself was a stark departure from the previous arrivals of his McCormack uncles and aunts who had simply gotten on a ship and showed up in America a half century earlier.

In order to receive a visa Paddy had to provide a financially responsible sponsor who was already an American citizen. His sponsor was an aunt, Bridget McKenna of West Orange who supplied the required affidavit of support and certification from her bank that she was financially solvent and a letter from the West Orange tax collector that her property tax payments were up to date. Having successfully navigated the relevant bureaucracy, Paddy received his visa in April 1948 and arrived in New Jersey in July of that year.[18]

Paddy married another Irish immigrant, Philomena Darcy, in 1958. They met in New York when her ship from Ireland arrived. Paddy had been there with her brother greeting other passengers. Over the next few years they had four children. He worked for a number of employers, including Turner Fencing in Hanover, where he was a foreman for twenty years. After a stroke in 1977, he eventually worked in maintenance at the East Orange General Hospital. In 1976 he and Mena became the owners of the Franklin Tavern in West Orange, which they sold in 1998, but continued to hold the mortgage. Paddy died in 2008.

Paddy's younger sister Maureen, born in 1933, came to the United States as a teenager in 1949 and found work as a child's private nurse. She lived at first in West Orange with her aunt, Kate Drury, and returned home in the summer of 1951 for a long visit. She met Albert LePochet at Mayfair Farms in West Orange, where they both worked, and they married in 1956. After her marriage Maureen continued to work for a while as a secretary and then spent most of the next decade as a homemaker, raising her four children. In 1968 she and Albert started a restaurant, La

---

17 Acknowledgement of P. McLoughlin's application for Immigration, American Consulate General, Dublin, 26 November 1947.
18 Letter of welcome to the United States, Watson Miller, Commisioner Immigration and Naturalization Service, to Patrick McLoughlin, 13 July 1948.

Montagne, in Rockaway Township, NJ. Tragically, Maureen died young in 1969 after a brief illness.

--

The children of the McCormack siblings who remained in Ireland faced many of the same economic hardships and lack of opportunity at home as had their parents, aunts and uncles decades earlier. The Anglo-Irish War and subsequent Civil War severely damaged the infrastructure of Ireland and set back its already crippled economy. The generation born between 1915 and 1933 lived in a land technically free of England, but still highly dependent on English trade and good will. It was abundantly clear that unless you were going to inherit the family farm, join the priesthood or other religious orders, your future was uncertain. The Irish Diaspora continued as once again family members seriously considered emigration. The impact of World War II on Ireland's prospects was particularly harsh, though it offered opportunities as well due to labor shortages in England. All three of Martin's daughters left for England to pursue their professional training during or immediately following the war, though two of them later returned, married farmers and settled back into a traditional Irish lifestyle. The choice of permanent emigration sent two of Margaret McLoughlin's children to the United States right after the war, seeking greater opportunities. They never returned except for visits. Surviving letters from the post-war period pessimistically speak of hard times in Ireland and gratitude for presents sent by relatives abroad. In the light of Ireland's prosperity at the end of the 20th century, one can easily forget that times were very hard just a generation earlier. These days, however, the collapse of the Irish real estate bubble and its effects on the economy Have once again ignited widespread emigration as "...abandoned housing projects rot, waist-high weeds sprouting from cracks in the sidewalks. The proportion of households without a working adult is the highest in the European Union, and thousands of

Irish continue to leave the country in search of work."[19] The oft-heard lament, "There is nothing here for anyone..." echoes again across the land.

[19] Suzanne Daley, "From Ireland to Greece: The New Fiscal Reality," *New York Times*, 2 Jan. 2013, A4.

J.P. McCormack 1982   *William A. McCormack 1914*

William P. McCormick 1917   *William J. McCormack 1909*

Thomas Callahan 1921

*Patrick and Andrew Callahan
1943*

*Bridget (Sr. Joseph)
McLoughlin 1939*

Patrick and Philomena McLoughlin Wedding 1958

Mai McCormack Robinson 1993

Epilogue
An American Funeral

Pak looked once again at the neatly typed and itemized bill he had received that day from E. B. Gifford: $770.00, with a promised discount of $34.25 if he paid it by January 31, 1953. It was all laid out plainly -- $15.00 for bringing Kate's body back to Chatham from Hudson Hospital, a further $590 for the funeral itself on December 31st, complete with hearse and concrete vault, and the remainder for various incidentals such as flowers, newspaper notices, opening and closing the grave, and a $16.00 fee to the priest for the Mass offering.

It had been mercifully quick. They quietly celebrated Kate's 76th birthday a month earlier, and some of the children traveled home for Christmas. But, the next day came the chest pains, the ambulance, and the hurried trip to Hudson. On the morning of the 28th she was gone. There had not been a wake; the children had discouraged it -- Where will people park? The house is just too small. No, father, that's not the way funerals are done here.... He had done what they wanted.

As he waited for his tea to cool a bit, Pak's mind drifted back to that day over fifty years earlier when Katie had come up from New Jersey with his sister Delia to Pittsfield. They had known each other as children back home, but he had not seen her since she was still an awkward teenager. Oh, how different she was now! He smiled as he remembered their brief courtship and even more as their long life together unfolded in his memory. He poured some tea into his saucer and stared at it for a long time. "I'll be 80 in August; what am I to do now?

Before replacing the neat bill in its equally neat envelope, Pak noted one final itemized expense: $4.00 for hairdressing. "Jesus, Mary and Joseph! We didn't pay much more than that to cross the Atlantic!"

I chose to limit this study to the generation of those McCormacks who came to America, their siblings who stayed home, and their children. My goal was to portray the family as a case study of the Irish Diaspora and to show how the McCormacks fared in turbulent times, both in Ireland and America. The first generation died out in 1970, and there are still two members of the second generation living, one in Ireland and one in England, both in their 90s. The last of their American counterparts died in 1993.

Now, of course, there are many living descendants – the grandchildren, great-grandchildren and great-great-grandchildren of Patrick and Catherine Keenan McCormack's offspring. The oldest are in their 80's and the youngest still in their cradles. The family has come a long way from its humble beginnings. It includes physicians, lawyers, professors and teachers, salespeople and entrepreneurs, just to name a few. The McCormack surname is now extinguished in Ireland, but continues here in the United States where they are all following the still mysterious family tradition of being named William.

I admit to being somewhat surprised by how closely the family adhered to the broad historical trends of Irish emigration and settlement. But, I suppose I should not have been since the "big picture" of history is always composed of small portraits. This branch of the McCormacks originated in the province of Connacht, which was the hardest hit by The Famine and the source of the highest percentage of population loss in the 19th century. So, the fact that over half of the generation born in the last half of the century left Ireland is unremarkable. That they settled on the east coast of the United States is also not surprising, given their arrival in New York City. Nor is it a shock that many of the men in the first and second generation of the family were policemen and railway workers, iconic occupations for Irishmen.

Over the years the McCormacks in America increasingly lost their identification as immigrants. One example of this trend can be seen in marriage patterns. Five of the six siblings who emigrated to America in the late 19th century married Irish spouses after they arrived. Their children, however, ranged farther afield in their courting. Of fifteen marriages in this next generation, ten were to spouses of non-Irish descent. Plus, those who did marry Irish were predominantly the older members of the generation. By my father's time, the Irish-American McCormacks had largely blended into the melting pot of America.

Those who remained at home also lived fairly stereotypical Irish lives as farmers – except William who chose a career in the Royal Irish Constabulary and, later, as a hotelier. Their children became farmers, teachers, nurses, a priest and a nun. No great surprises here. We also know from letters sent from Ireland to America that the emigrants often sent money home to other family members. Remittances and gifts continued throughout the period, even as late as the mid-1950's, when Margaret McCormack McLoughlin, the youngest of the emigrants' siblings, mentioned in a letter to her daughter in America that her older sister Bridget had sent her $3.00 for Christmas. "I didn't fare badly," she concluded.[1]

In 1852 as thousands of desperate Irish fled their homeland in the wake of The Famine, the *New York Times* published an article titled "Ireland in America."[2] It noted that over the previous four days alone twelve thousand people had arrived in New York City and that every recent year had seen more than 300,000 "...souls, a city almost as large as Philadelphia ... emptied from ships upon the New York docks."[3] Not only would this huge influx of people have a profound effect on America, the author noted, but an even greater impact on Ireland, where a third of the population had "...either perished from the famine, or ... were driven from their native land" over the past decade. Though the math is not quite right, the article clearly recognized that a huge population shift, later called the Irish Diaspora, had begun. The article goes on to lambaste, in great detail, the British policies which had magnified the Irish calamity and concluded with two predictions, borne out at least in part over the past century and a half. First, the author notes:

---

[1] Letter, Margaret McLoughlin to Maureen McLoughlin 22 January 1955. Collection of McLoughlin family.
[2] "Ireland in America," *New York Times*, 2 April 1852.
[3] Ibid.

When men leave their homes for a foreign shore, merely because they hope to improve their condition, they retain grateful recollections of the land they have left. It is still home to them, and has strong ties upon their affection. But when men are driven away by unjust laws – by starvation and the fear of death – when they are forced to snatch their wives and children, and take them three thousand miles across the sea, to save them from the jaws of famine, while they see plenty and luxury all around them – their memories of home become motives of hatred, and will feed the fires which time cannot quench.[4]

Though the immigrants continued to love Ireland, this is a fairly prescient prediction of their attitude toward England which developed over the next century. The second prediction is particularly telling:

There is no hope for Ireland under the present state of things ... Emigration, desperate and hard as it is, seems to be the only resource of the Irish people. Transplantation to the United States is all the chance of growth that is left to them. They cannot here, of course, preserve for many generations their nationality. But they can do what is much more important for themselves and their children – they can take deep root in this soil, and grow up with the vigorous and fruitful American tree...[5]

The saga of the McCormacks and their neighbors personifying the unfolding Irish Diaspora bears witness to the truths contained in this early article which chronicles its beginning. In 1852 the anonymous *Times* reporter could not have seen that the panicked Famine-era emigration was nearing its end, only to be replaced by many decades of less overwhelming, but relentlessly steady transplantation of the Irish to America. The balance between "push" and "pull" shifted significantly to the latter, and the typical immigrant was now young and single. Nevertheless,

---

[4] Ibid.
[5] Ibid.

they did come bearing grudges against England, and over the following generations many of their descendants lost touch with their ethnicity and their homeland. But, as I discovered as I researched this book, the Americans' Irish roots were indeed deep and could be nourished once again. When I travelled to the "homeplace" in Frenchpark to begin my research in Ireland in 2010, my cousin John Dowd, a farmer much like J. P. McCormack who we met there in 1982, greeted me with the question "How long are you home for?" It felt good.

Appendix 1: Vital Statistics

Parents

- Patrick McCormack b. 1833. Married Catherine Keenan. 12 February 1861; d. 16 March 1900
- Catherine Keenan McCormack b. 1842. Married Patrick McCormack 12 February 1861; d. 2 July 1915

Children

1. John McCormack b. 31 March, 1862; Married Anne Morrisroe, 6 December 1888; d. 17 October 1937
2. Patrick McCormack b. 5 March 1864; d. before March, 1866
3. Patrick McCormack b. 10 March 1866; Married Delia Callaghan, 6 January 1892; d. 8 August 1897
4. James McCormack b. 25 March 1868; Never married; d. 11 May 1946
5. Thomas McCormack b. 18 March 1870; Married Annie Hoare 25 April 1900; d. 2 June 1938.
6. Michael McCormack b. 16 April 1872; Married Helen Agnes Higgins 3 September 1900; d. 26 January 1941
7. William McCormack b. 14 September 1874. Married Eliza Creamer 14 February 1916; d. 1939/40
8. Catherine T. McCormack b. 11 December 1876. Married Patrick J. Callahan, 6 September 1899; d. 28 December 1952
9. Thadeus McCormack b. 16 January 1879; d. ?
10. Martin McCormack b. 31 March 1882. Married May Ann Giblin 1918; d. 24 December 1958.
11. Beatrice McCormack* b. 9 October 1883; Married Ernest Daniels 1901-1903; d. 22 October 1970
12. Margaret McCormack. b. 1886. Married Thomas McLoughlin., 1916; d. 12 November 1955

*Birth registered as Bridget McCormack in 1883; appears in 1901 Irish census as Delia McCormack; appears in 1910 and subsequent US censuses as Beatrice Daniels and known to family as Beatrice or Bea

138

Grandchildren

- *John McCormick [3/31/1862–10/17/1937] - Anne Morrisroe [2/20/1860–12/21/1942]*
1. Winifred K McCormick b. 14 May 1890. Married Matthew O'Connell [1879-1946], 1909, d. 6/30/1948
2. John McCormick b. 15 April 1892, d. 26 August 1893
3. Anne Beatrice McCormick b. 18 October 1894. d. 26 October 1952
4. Thomas S. McCormick b. 17 December 1896. Married Barbara M Smith [?]; Married Loretta Samuelson Burns 1 October 1929. Married Mary Maguire [?]. d. July 1975
5. Mary Rose McCormick b. 24 September 1899. Married Robert Emmet Morrison [1893-?] 1924. d. May 1989
6. Margaret Cecilia McCormick b. 4 April 1902. d. 25 April 1964
7. William Patrick McCormick b. 5 December 1904. Married Rosemary Vukan 20 January 1947. d. 1 January 1984

- *Patrick McCormack [3/10/1866-8/8/1897] - Delia Callaghan [9/15/1868-2/24/1947]*
1. Thomas Melvin McCormack b. 19 January 1893. d. 6 March 1929
2. Patrick Joseph McCormack b. 24 January 1894. d. 1900-1910
3. William Andrew McCormack b. 7 December 1895. Married Mary Estelle Hayes [1905-1994] 3 August 1929. d. 30 March 1991
4. Mary Agnes [Mollie] McCormack b. 17 January 1897. d. January 1980

- *James McCormack [3/25/1868–5/11/1946]   Never Married*

- *Thomas McCormack [3/18/1870–6/2/1938] - Annie Hoare [4/25/1873 – 2/4/1948]*
1. William J. McCormack b. 12 July 1902. Married Loretta Vreeland 3 October 1929. d. 3 April 1984.

- *Michael J. McCormack [4/16/1872–1/26/1941] - Helen Agnes Higgins [11/29/1876–11/7/1918]*
1. Mary A. McCormack b. 1902. d. ?
2. Catherine McCormack b. 1903. d. c. 1980
3. John McCormack b.10 May 1906. d. 19 June 1944

- *William McCormack [9/14/1874–1939/40] - Eliza Creamer [9/28/1868–c. 1935]*
No Children

- *Catherine T. McCormack [12/11/1876–12/28/1952] - Patrick Callahan [8/3/1873-2/7/1957]*
1. Madeline Callahan b. 19 July 1900. d. 24 February 1978
2. William John Callahan b. 1903. Married Cora Mohan 30 April 1928. d. 20 June 1964
3. Augustine Callahan b. 1905. Married Evelyn Gardner 21 June 1925. d. 16 January 1981
4. Thomas Callahan b. 4 October 1907. Married Evelyn Colby 3 April 1944. d. 4 January 1993
5. Andrew R. Callahan b. 20 September 1909. d. 5 August 1955
6. Mary V. Callahan b. 26 November 1911. d. 27 May 1979
7. Robert E. Callahan b. 11 January 1914. Married Mary Cook 18 September 1937. d. 25 November 1962
8. Timothy J. Callahan b. 7 January 1919. d. 23 January 1969
9. Eleanor Callahan b. 14 June 1921. d. 15 September 1979.

- *Martin McCormack [03/31/1882-12/24/1958] - Mary Ann Giblin [02/14/1888 –7/8/1962]*
1. Mary Jane [Mai] McCormack Robinson b. 4 September 1921. Married Arnold Robinson [3/3/1903 - 4/14/1995] 09/24/1959.
2. Margaret McCormack Carty b. 19 June 1923. Married Michael Carty July, 1958. d. 26 September 1978
3. John P. McCormack b. 10 July 1924. d. 15 September 2001
4. Bridget Theresa [Beatie] McCormack Dowd b. 5 June 1927 Married Tim Dowd 1952. d. 9 April 2005.
5. William Joseph McCormack b. 11 December 1928. d. 22 March 1951.

- *Bridget [Beatrice] McCormack [10/9/1883–10/11/1970] - Ernest Daniels [1883-?]*
1. Ernest William Daniels, b. 15 January 1911. Married Frances ? [year?]. d. 14 April 1992
2. William Joseph Daniels b. 10 February 1914. Married Mary Brady [Year ?]. d. November 1974
3. Mary E. Daniels b. 4 October 1920. Married Harry Franklin/?? Prococco [years?]. d. 11 October 1968

- *Margaret McCormack [1886-11/12/1955] - Thomas McLoughlin [12/16/1943]*
1. Matthew McLoughlin b. 4 June 1915. d. 4 June 2000
2. Katie McLoughlin b. 2 November 1917. Married John Reynolds, 5 April 1942. d. 12 July 2010
3. John McLoughlin b. 1919. Married Ellie Noon 195?. d. 30 September 1982
4. Bridget [Sr. Joseph] McLoughlin b.16 November 1922
5. Maggie McLoughlin b. 11April 1925. Married John Allen, March 1950. d. 21 September 1994
6. Patrick McLoughlin b. 29 May 1927. Married Philomena Darcy, 12 April 1958. d. 11 May 200
7. Maureen McLoughlin b. 18 June 1933. Married Albert LePochat 24 April 1956. d. 24 December 1969

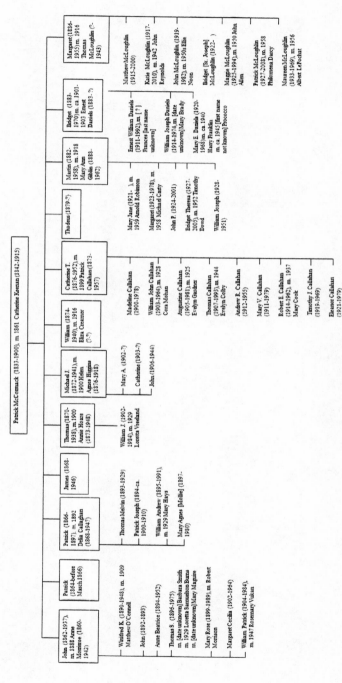

Appendix 2: Family Tree

This page is intentionally blank

CPSIA information can be obtained at www.ICGtesting.com
Printed in the USA
LVOW06s1104101215

466254LV00001B/25/P